To Beloved son Richard
Dahan

ROOT SPEAKS TO BUD

With eternal love,

Subham & Pat

ROOT SPEAKS TO BUD

Fulfilling the Purpose of Life

by

William Hassan Suhrawardi Gebel

Sulūk Press
Omega Publications
New Lebanon New York

Published by Sulūk Press,
an imprint of Omega Publications, Inc.
New Lebanon NY
www.omegapub.com

Cover photograph © Shutterstock.com
Cover design by Sandra Lillydahl

Excerpts from *Working: People Talk About What They Do All Day and How They Feel About What They Do*
Copyright © 1996 by Studs Terkel, The New Press.
www.thenewpress.com

This edition is printed on acid-free paper that meets ANSI standard X39–48.

Gebel, William L. Hassan Suhrawardi (1941–)
Root Speaks to Bud; Fulfilling the Purpose of Life
Includes preface, notes on author, index.
1. Gebel, William Hassan Suhrawardi
2. Sufism 3. Psychology—Self-actualization II. Title

Library of Congress Control Number: 2015942164

Printed and bound in the United States of America
ISBN 978–1–941810–118

Contents

A shoot will grow out of Jesse's root stock,
a bud will sprout from his roots.

—Isaiah 11:1

O Thou, the root of my life's plant,
Thou wert hidden so long
in my bud-like soul.
But now Thou hast come out,
O my life's fruit,
after the blossoming of my heart.

—Hazrat Inayat Khan[1]

"The Pressure Flow Hypothesis is the best-supported theory to explain the movement of food through the phloem, living tissue of a tree just inside the bark. It was proposed by Ernst Munch, a German plant physiologist, in 1930."

A high concentration of organic sugar inside cells of the phloem at a sugar-producing source, such as the root, creates a pressure that draws water into the cells. The resulting hydrostatic pressure then causes the phloem's sap to move to the plant's many growing areas, such as the buds.[2]

---

1 Inayat Khan, *The Complete Sayings of Hazrat Inayat Khan* (New Lebanon: Omega Publications, 1978), 63.
2 "Pressure Flow Hypothesis," (Wikipedia. http://en.wikipedia.org/wiki/Pressure_Flow_Hypothesis).

PREFACE

THIS book is an attempt to share, in contemporary language, the wisdom of Sufism on the theme of life's meaning. Sufi contemplatives have dived deep into life's mysteries and emerged with an illuminated understanding. As my primary source for the wisdom of Sufism, I have taken the profound teachings of Hazrat Inayat Khan, an Indian master musician and Sufi mystic, who brought Sufism to the West in 1910. His teachings have been collected in the fourteen volumes of *The Sufi Message* and, in a more scholarly version, as *The Complete Works of Pir-O-Murshid Hazrat Inayat Khan*.[1]

I have had the great blessing of spending years in the inspiring presence of Hazrat Inayat Khan's son Pir Vilayat Inayat Khan, and grandson Pir Zia Inayat-Khan. Whatever understanding of the wisdom of Sufism I have gained, I owe to their brilliant teachings and patient guidance.

Writing this book is a piece of the puzzle that is my purpose in life. From childhood I was drawn to writing and throughout my life I dreamed of fulfilling a destiny as a writer. Writing was so important to me that,

---

1 Hazrat Inayat Khan, *The Sufi Message* series (Netherlands: Servire, 1979); *The Complete Works of Pir-O-Murshid Hazrat Inayat Khan* (New Lebanon, NY: Omega Publications/Nekbakht Foundation).

ironically, I feared to pursue it because the risk of failing at it was too much to bear.

My career path has been a patchwork of divergent roads, seemingly taken at random. I have been an assistant professor of astrophysics, a member of a theater company, a technical writer, a psychotherapist, and a spiritual guide. Gradually I came to see that each new direction I took was preparing me for the dream I never abandoned. My confidence grew and I opened up to emotional and spiritual dimensions previously latent.

In writing this book I have had to grapple with a continuing struggle with my ego. My fear of failure reared its head once again. The perverse nature of the ego *no* summoned dreams of glory, aggravating self-criticism and threatening me with writer's block. Through periods of darkness, the teachings I wish to share have come to my rescue. They have reminded me that my purpose is not a selfish personal wish for success and recognition, but, on a personal level, the wish to contribute to an awakening of consciousness whose time I believe has come. And from another point of view, my *no proof* purpose, like the purpose of each soul, is driven by a mysterious wish arising at the very source of life.

My method of working is what the Sufis call *contemplation*. For the Sufis contemplation means holding an idea in the mind, clearing away preconceptions about it, remaining empty, and waiting for the many facets of the idea to reveal themselves.

yes To prepare for contemplation, it is first valuable to practice concentration, the ability to hold the mind steady and focused. Steadiness of mind seems to be connected with steadiness of the glance. By focusing your glance on an object, ideally one that holds your attention by its beauty, and bringing your glance back again and again when your attention wanders, you are strengthening a faculty of unwavering focus. When you are able to hold your mind firmly on an object, you are ready to focus on an idea. The idea is self-revealing, but if your mind wanders, you won't have a chance to receive what the idea discloses.

The ideas and insights in the teachings of Hazrat Inayat Khan are deep and resonant. Reading them sparks deep memories and enlightening reflections on one's life and experiences. I have tried to absorb these teachings mentally and also to digest them by putting them into practice in my life. Through the process of contemplation, my hope is to express these ideas anew in a contemporary voice.

I am taking liberties by filtering Sufi insights through my limited understanding. I'm also embellishing the wisdom of Sufism with contemporary ideas and, sometimes, novelties that have come through my contemplative process.

For these digressions and interpretations I take responsibility and offer at the start, my apologies for misrepresentations and distortions. I take consolation in the thought that Sufis have always been free thinkers, sharing what they have culled from inner experience.

Part I

Root and Bough

INTRODUCTION

MOST of us lead busy lives. If we are fortunate to live a privileged life in a prosperous country, our time is filled with responsibilities of family, career, and citizenry. Living in a poor nation, the challenges of survival may be all-consuming. What time is there to consider the larger questions in life?

My life is passing quickly. Before long, I may be asking myself, *Did I do what I came here to do?* If we had time to ponder the meaning of life, we would be faced with the age-old questions: Is there any meaning in life? Why am I here?

In a Stanford commencement address, Steve Jobs talked about a close brush with death. He called death "very likely the single best invention of life. It is life's change agent. It clears out the old to make way for the new." He continued with this advice for the graduating class:

> Your time is limited, so don't waste it living someone else's life. Don't be trapped by dogma, which is living with the results of other people's thinking. Don't let the noise of other's opinions drown out your own inner voice. And most importantly, have the courage to follow your heart and

3

intuition. They somehow already know what you truly want to become. Everything else is secondary.[1]

In an age dominated by the proliferation of scientific discovery, it seems natural to frame the question of meaning in scientific terms: Is life a meaningless by-product of evolutionary influences, jostling for survival? And is the push to survive simply a result of naturally selected, biochemical processes that somehow stumbled across a way to propagate themselves? Is our experience only the further propagation of countless random novelties refined by natural selection?

In the framework of our human experience, in its largest context, we find our lives to be a tiny whisper in a vast expanse of space and time. I am one among billions of fellow humans on the planet, each, like me, a whole world of knowledge and experience.

There is much in our lives that we may consider meaningful. If we are raising healthy and thriving children or contributing to the larger society, we may justly feel some satisfaction. And yet there is a nagging feeling that there is something important we are supposed to be doing, and we have become bogged down in the routine of our daily lives. When our time is up, will we feel that we did what we came here to do?

Walter Lundquist, a middle-aged industrial designer interviewed by Studs Terkel for his book *Working*, told his story about awakening to the question of meaning and doing something about it. The death of his father was a turning point in his life. Listening to his father lament about missing life's opportunities jolted him into reassessing his own career. It became clear to him

---

1 Steve Jobs, Stanford Commencement Address, June 12, 2005.

that he was squandering his time and abilities on priorities he didn't believe in. He began to find volunteer or low-paying jobs that were meaningful and satisfying. He was faced with a big decision, how to survive doing the work that he cared about.

> I'm straddling two worlds and I'm trying to move over into the sane one. But I can't make a living out of it. . .
>
> I'm struggling to survive. I'm running out of funds. I may have to pimp again for survival's sake. But I'll not give up the sane work. I'm scurrying about. If it doesn't work, I may do somewhat what young people do and drop out. I'll stop existing in this society. I'll work on a road crew. I'll cut lumber or whatever the hell it'll be. But I'll never again play the full-time lying dishonest role I've done most of my life.
>
> Once you wake up the human animal you can't put it back to sleep again.[2]

Is there an answer to the basic question of whether life has any meaning? I don't have a general answer, but I believe that you have an answer for your life, and every life has its own answer.

[handwritten: I do!]

To find this answer for yourself is the adventure of life, an exploration into uncharted territory. It means entering a wild realm which science has been unable to penetrate. Although the way is difficult, it is open to anyone who chooses to take up the challenge.

[handwritten: maybe / maybe not / ↓ unfounded]

---

2 Studs Terkel, *Working: People Talk about What They Do All Day and How They Feel about What They Do* (New York: The New Press, 1972), 526–27.

Hidden Treasure

TEAR down this house. A hundred thousand new houses can be built from the transparent yellow carnelian buried beneath it, and the only way to get to that is to do the work of demolishing and then digging under the foundations.

With that value in hand all the new construction will be done without effort.

And anyway, sooner or later this house will fall on its own. The jewel treasure will be uncovered, but it won't be yours then. The buried wealth is your pay for doing the demolition, the pick and shovel work. If you wait and just let it happen, you'd bite your hand and say, "I didn't do as I knew I should have."

This is a rented house. You don't own the deed. You have a lease, and you've set up a little shop, where you barely make a living sewing patches on torn clothing. Yet only a few feet underneath are two veins, pure red and bright gold carnelian.

Quick! Take the pickaxe and pry the foundation.

You've got to quit this seamstress work. What does the patch-sewing mean, you ask. Eating and drinking. The heavy cloak of the body is always getting torn. You patch it with food, and other restless ego-satisfactions.

> *Rip up one board from the shop floor and look into*
> *the basement. You'll see two glints in the dirt.*
> —Jelaluddin Rumi[1]

[handwritten margin notes: good, a but, e explain]

What are we seeking? We are used to looking outward when we ask ourselves this question. We expect to find what we are seeking out there, somewhere. If we are fortunate that the survival needs of those who depend on us are secure, then we might seek conventional goals: wealth and influence, adventure and creativity, friendship and community, success in business or profession, service to a cause or to those in need, artistic expression, scientific exploration or invention, raising a healthy family. We look outward for satisfaction and happiness.

This outward work can be genuine, admirable, and satisfying. The poet Rumi dismisses it as seamstress work, the attention that our ego self demands to supply its needs. Jesus said that we should not worry about the things our ego self needs such as food and clothing. He was alerting us to something of much greater value. "Seek ye first the kingdom of God and His righteousness, and all these things shall be added to you."[2]

[handwritten margin notes: not exactly; referring? seems outside oneself if not explicit]

Rumi is saying something similar. There is a treasure to be found in our basement. To find it means tearing down the house. It means challenging oneself to set aside the demands of the ego self for attention. We can turn our attention instead toward something that inspires and uplifts us.

There is an inner world and an outer world. We are used to paying attention to the outer world. We gen-

[handwritten margin notes: ego can be wind in the sale?]

1 Jelaluddin Rumi, *The Essential Rumi*, trans. Coleman Barks (New York: Harper Collins, 1996), 113–14.
2 Matthew 6:33.

erally think of the inner world as idle thoughts and fantasies. But we probably haven't given the inner world a chance to reveal its nature. What do we already know about the inner life? It has many layers. Our public and private thoughts come from inside. We have an emotional inner life. There is a psychological layer that hosts our neuroses and obsessions. We are probably aware of insights and intuitions that come to us spontaneously from within. Our dream life is part of our inner life. You may feel occasionally that you receive guidance from within for difficult decisions in life. Perhaps we take all of this for granted and don't think about cultivating that resource, which seems to operate on its own. Our inner life may be masked by psychological turmoil or diminished by doubt — Rumi's basement dirt.

Rumi tells us to rip up a board to look into the basement. There may be a gentler way to gain access to our inner life. To get a glimpse of the basement, we have to learn how to enter the silence. You may not know how to enter the silence. In social interactions, silence is often uncomfortable. We take it as a gap in the conversation, as an embarrassing lack of something to say. Sitting down, closing your eyes, and being silent, your mind may feel obligated to fill the empty space with babble. You may feel uncomfortable with emptiness. The inner world could seem barren and dull compared to the rich stimuli of the outer world.

But hidden in the silence is a peek at the treasure Rumi speaks of. It may be that the gems don't stick up out of the dirt. Finding them may require some digging into the layer of psychological turmoil. Don't be discouraged or lose patience. The treasure is a clear understanding of your purpose for being here. When that

8

purpose becomes clear, life takes on meaning. Light comes into your eyes. You have something worthwhile to accomplish. The treasure is not only a revelation of our purpose but also a resource for discovering how to accomplish it.

INNER KNOWLEDGE

Yes - glorious recipient ✗

I have not come to teach what you know not;
I have come to deepen in you that wisdom which is
yours already.

— Hazrat Inayat Khan[1]

WE seek knowledge outwardly. We study books, the accumulated knowledge of the ages. We learn from teachers or mentors. We examine the world by keen observation or by experiment. We learn from experience. But there is an inner knowing that already belongs to us. It is mostly hidden from our view by our assumptions and concepts. The mystics say that you have to unlearn what you have learned outwardly. In order to gain access to inner knowing, you have to put aside what you think you know, become open *yes* and receptive, learn to relax mind and body, and listen carefully.

Our style of life has become so stimulated and speeded up that we may quickly become bored and impatient with silence and peace. Stimulation has its price. There is a kind of exhaustion of the nerves that follows excitation. To gain the pleasure of stimulation the next time, the intensity needs to increase. Our nervous system is being progressively dulled. You may have noticed

1 Hazrat Inayat Khan, *The Complete Sayings of Hazrat Inayat Khan* (New Lebanon, NY: Omega Publications, 2005), 112.

that the intensity of stimulation in popular media has steadily increased over the years. Fortunately the nervous system seems to have some power of recovery. If you take a vacation from stimulation for a period of time, you become resensitized. Exposing yourself to popular media again feels overwhelming until you adapt and reenter the norm.

If we consider our usual state to be one of intoxication from a potent mix of media, stimulants in food and entertainment, and constant feeding of the mind, then we could imagine adopting a gradual program of sobriety. This means training yourself to do without stimulation and learning to enjoy peace, solitude, and relaxation: a more natural state.

The knowledge of the inner world is the knowledge of self. It is not a knowledge of the mind but a knowledge of the heart. It is a knowledge that comes through feeling.

We have learned through experience that the world is a hard place where the trusting heart is betrayed. We have been criticized, belittled, and humiliated. Our hearts have been broken by rejection or hostility. To protect the heart from further pain, we have put a hard shell around it, sealing off our finer, tender feelings; and adopting a mask of toughness and indifference. By deadening the heart, we hope to avoid the despair of further wounding.

Yet our life depends on the flow of love. We resort to intense stimulation to experience some sensation in our fortress heart. We enjoy the love of family and friends yet feel loneliness, isolation, and fear of rejection if we let down our guard.

Entering the inner world of silence then, is not only an act of sobriety but also an act of courage and faith. What will you find if you penetrate the thick walls of the fortress and return to the pure innocent heart of childhood? Do you remember the wonder of discovering the magic of life as a child? Can you get in touch with a feeling of purity and sacredness? Are you prepared to open your heart in spite of the risks? There is good reason to do this. A completely new world can open up.

In Studs Terkel's *Working*, Carmelita Lester tells a story of a miraculous healing that opened up her heart and changed her life. She was working as a nurse. Then one day, mysteriously, she lost all her strength and couldn't walk. She couldn't feed herself. She was helpless. Many doctors examined her but couldn't find a cure. Her primary doctor told her that she had to live with it; there was nothing medicine could do. So she turned to prayer and prayed with all her flagging strength.

Then one night, spontaneously, an electric shock went through her legs. And in the morning she regained a little movement. The shocks came again for two more nights and to her joyful amazement she was able to walk again.

Her life as a nurse was transformed by her unexpected recovery.

> I was a nurse before, but I wasn't devoted. I saw how they treated people when I was there. Oh, it was pitiful. I couldn't stand it. And from that, I have tender feelings. That changed me. That's when I decided to devote myself.
>
> I feel sorry for everybody who cannot help themselves. For that reason I never rest.[2]

The heart is the seat of intuition. When the heart opens, knowledge comes that is prior to thinking. You

2 Terkel, *Working*, 503–4.

gain an understanding and a sympathy for others. The walls of separation are breached and you feel more at home in the world. As long as you were busy protecting yourself, the world seemed dangerous and threatening. When you see that we are all in the same boat, that others share your fragility, you extend your sphere of protection to include them. That boundary can be extended further and further.

King Solomon was granted a wish by the Holy One. He asked for an understanding heart. Because his request was humble and wise, he was granted all the power and wealth he might have asked for. With an understanding heart comes the knowledge of how to make the best of life. Inner knowledge offers intuition and guidance. In the silence you can see your purpose more clearly and find the wherewithal to accomplish it.

Ignorance is often portrayed as darkness. The knowledge that comes from opening the heart and turning within is like a light that cuts through darkness. When that light dawns, the shadows of doubt, self-absorption, and limitation begin to fade.

Meaning in Life

In Western culture, education prepares you to seek a career, find a partner, raise a family, and be a responsible citizen. Many find meaning in this way of life, taking pride in work or in being of service, finding satisfaction in relationships, enjoying the maturing of children, taking part in a community and the life of a nation. For some, the expected role of responsible citizen may be lacking something. Perhaps one feels that some talent is lying dormant, not being fully utilized. For others the typical social role might feel stifling. One may nurse a desire that seems unrealistic or self-indulgent. Then one puts it off or gives up on it.

Some indigenous cultures, notably the Native American culture, have initiation ceremonies in which a youth takes a vision quest. Separated from social supports, alone with the self, the youth observes the signs that nature gives in answer to prayer and intentionality. The ceremony is a sober commitment to seeking guidance for a lifetime. The experiences the youth has are interpreted by a tribal elder who has spent a lifetime cultivating intuition and insight. What is revealed about meaning and purpose is sealed by giving a spiritual name and making a shield. Symbols are emblazoned on the shield to remind the youth of the sacred purpose. Thus each individual has a unique purpose disclosed by the natural world as interpreted by the wisdom of the elders. The needs of the tribe accommodate the role of the individual, finding a way for that person to contribute according to that person's purpose.

Lacking the tribal structure that can adjust itself to each person's purpose, and lacking an education which prepares each person to seek their unique role early in life, our social structure makes it difficult to find a deeper meaning outside of typical social roles.

Whereas a member of a tribe can rely on the community to acknowledge and support meaning and purpose, in Western society one who strikes out to fulfill a unique purpose may be labeled a dreamer. A successful person might be admired, but on the way to success, one must have courage, determination, and faith.

The scientific view of the world has arisen from an attitude of skepticism. That which I will accept as real is what can be demonstrated by experiment, can be perceived by the senses, and is explained through reason. Life is material existence played out according to material causes, which appear to arise through chance. The universe has evolved according to physical laws that simply are. They are revealed by keen observation of physical phenomena. They have no inherent meaning. The implication is that our lives have no meaning but are the outcome of indifferent forces, mindlessly running on the rails of natural laws.

Ironically, scientists find meaning in discovering how nature works. There is an aesthetic dimension to scientific research. The scientist is moved by the elegance of the working of nature. The intricacy and complexity and interdependency found in the natural world elicits a feeling of awe and appreciation.

So there is a feeling of meaningfulness that scientists experience, which cannot be accounted for in a strictly material world. A thoroughgoing scientist might point to the source of emotional life in specific areas of the brain. Yet how a sense of meaningfulness arises cannot be explained by brain chemicals and nerve firings.

Many find meaning in their religious faith. The pursuits of everyday life become meaningful in a larger sacred context. Satisfaction may come through prayer and worship, through the warmth of a religious community, by aspiring to live up to religious values, and by selfless service to family, community, or those in need, both near and far. You may discover meaning and purpose through religious experience as a Christian, Jew, Muslim, or practitioner of another religion.

The experience of meaning or the absence of meaning is apparent. Meaning gives motivation to life and its absence leaves one feeling dull or depressed.

You might say that a scientist is motivated by a desire for knowledge and a religious person by a desire to serve God and serve others. What is your motivation? What is your desire? Knowing your desire and making a decision to follow that desire brings meaning into your life.

The hidden treasure glinting in the basement of your inner life is the revelation of your desire. It is what you are meant to do in life.

good question

16

WHO AM I?

WHERE does this sense of myself as a separate individual, with a body, mind, and feelings, come from? We come into the world in a pure state: innocent, open, defenseless. A newborn has no separate sense of identity. Margaret Mahler, an Object Relations psychologist, by making insightful observations of young children, followed the development of the sense of individuality through its stages of separation from the mother or caregiver. She identified the stage when separation becomes conscious at around the age of two.

Scientists studying the articulation of neurons and proliferation of synapses in the brain of the child have shed light on the influence of experience on the development of the brain and, therefore, on the sense of self. As the child is learning at the age of two its independence from the mother or caregiver, its experiences are strengthening certain neural pathways and neglected pathways are being pruned. Our emerging identity is shaped by experience.

Genetic inheritance, clearly seen in who we resemble, provides a framework of tendencies and sensitivities. To some degree we are a continuation of our parents and ancestors.

In adolescence, we develop self-consciousness. The tensions and stresses of social life contribute to a secret inner emotional life. Feelings of loneliness and isolation ensue.

When it comes time to separate from family and take responsibility as an adult, our sense of self shifts again. We struggle with the question, *where do I fit in*? We are faced with expectations from family, with the well-trodden pathway of the norms of society, with the encouragements and restrictions that others have impressed on us. Weighed against what others expect of us are rising interests, desires, and passions, and also self-doubts.

We may rebel against expectations or we may conform, either embracing or resigning ourselves to the choices made by others. In either case our sense of self has to broaden beyond the role we have played in the family.

As we take on more responsibility we become more aware of our limitations. The inner critical voice that was preoccupied with fitting in as a teenager now becomes the voice of negativity that highlights for us those aspects of our self-concept that we reject. We are more apt to dwell on our faults and mistakes than on our strengths and virtues.

Abraham Lincoln said that all actions are selfish, but some are wisely selfish while others are foolishly selfish. We hope that maturity will mellow us from self-absorbed and selfish actions to more considerate and caring actions. At some point in our development we begin to see our mistakes and limitations. If we can free ourselves from the emotional bind of reacting to this faultfinding, we can learn from our shortcomings and begin a lifelong process of seeking to live up to an ideal of how we would like to be. When improvements start to take hold, we gain confidence in the process; and self-examination becomes more comfortable. We develop more objectivity toward our personality or sense of self. As we see ourselves more objectively, we discover a greater calm and peace. We accept our limitations as part of the package and something to work with, rather than *that's just the way I am.*

Gradually we begin to see that the self we thought we were is a social construct. It has no inherent reality. The only thing that is real and reliable about oneself is the *I* that looks out through our eyes. The body and mind are constantly changing; and the aspects of personality are also shifting and changeable.

You wonder, *who am I really?* I thought I was a unique person distinct and separate from every other person and object. But the person I was a year ago is gone, and the person I am now will be gone tomorrow. There is something in our continually shifting experience that feels unchanging. It is hard to put your finger on it. Can you imagine stripping away every aspect of yourself that is subject to change: body, mind, feelings, sensations, point of view? Is there anything left? Yes, there is the bare sense of *I*, a witnessing consciousness that seems to look out at the world through my eyes. It has always been there and through all the changes in life it has remained the same. It seems ageless. There seems to be no quality to describe it other than *awareness* and *awakeness*. If it has any quality at all, one could call it *intelligence*. Can you imagine pure intelligence without any associated knowledge? You might say it is an ability to perceive and understand, but in potential, not yet in action. See if you can experience pure intelligence not as a concept but as an impression.

Is my intelligence distinct and different from the intelligence that peers through the eyes of others?

Let's leave this question open for now.

Trust and Faith

WHAT if you are carrying a heavy burden in life? It might be a burden of fear, worry, or insecurity. What if your heart has been broken and the wound hasn't healed? What if you are overtaken by grief or guilt or shame? Do such conditions slam the door on the promise of finding meaning and purpose?

Nothing in life is ever final. Your condition or situation might seem fixed and immovable. Facing fears squarely might feel overwhelming. But if you could step away from those feelings and see yourself objectively as though you were seeing another person going through your experience, a new perspective might open up. You might discover that what you are going through is a test that could potentially bring out dormant strengths.

Routine and comfort can deaden the heart and lull you into sleepwalking your way through life. Pain and struggle often bring about growth. A living heart, despite the pain of vulnerability, is capable of appreciating the scope of life's joys and sorrows much more fully than a heart that is protected but shut down.

Fear and insecurity block one from taking the risks necessary for building confidence. A broken heart can mend, and you can take the risk to love again. Grief can be assimilated if you fully embrace it. Guilt can be assuaged by finding a way to make amends. Shame, when acknowledged, brings you out of the shadows into the flawed human family and can ripen as humility.

The heart is remarkably resilient. However, pain is the medicine that restores the heart. If pain is resisted, or if you cling to it, the heart can become stuck. Then it closes or becomes bitter. Pain is dynamic. If it is to do its work, it can't be controlled. Opening the heart to pain is an act of surrender. Some wounds never heal fully, but the willingness to accept the pain can ennoble the heart. It can become sensitive, receptive, and more loving.

Finding meaning and purpose in life depends on cultivating an open heart. Intuition, guidance, and trust rely on the heart becoming soft and pliable. Therefore the trials you go through in life, in the long run, help you to find your way.

Self-confidence can develop when you take a risk, moving beyond the barriers of feeling stuck. Just trying something new brings relief and hope. Success makes you bolder and builds strength for further risk-taking.

What if you have a burden of responsibility that leaves no time for the adventure of life? Caring for children, or a family member with a serious illness, or for an aging parent, for example, may require all of your available time and energy. You want to give your attention freely to this kind of service. But if you feel tugged by a dream, an unfulfilled desire, it might be hard to give yourself fully to the demands of duty. Once again a shift in perspective might help to make your burden lighter. The challenges of caring for others can bring out latent strengths, especially if you can be fully present and give yourself willingly. By opening the heart and relying on its resourcefulness, you are taking steps that prepare you for working toward your goal when you are free to pursue it.

You may doubt that help can be attracted by your need. By praying, we articulate our need. Are prayers answered? Often they are, but not necessarily in the way we anticipated. A prayer might be answered in an unexpected way that turns out to be better than what we asked for. If you take a risk relying on unseen help, and help comes, your faith grows. You begin to trust that you don't have to carry your burdens by yourself. It doesn't matter what you call that help—serendipity, guardian angel, God, or luck. The great discovery is to gain confidence in an underlying benevolence. This faith not only helps to relieve stress and lighten the load you carry, but it is essential when setting out to find out what your life is about.

Our sense of whether the world is trustworthy or not is formed in infancy. Eric Erickson identified the first stage of psychological development as occurring in the first year of life. The infant finds its environment either safe and reliable or not so. Erickson called the healthy achievement of this stage basic trust.

Seeking your purpose requires development of basic trust. If your early experience was one of basic mistrust, then you have some serious remedial work to do. Your efforts to take risks, accept failures for the sake of learning, and have faith in prayer and hope will be more difficult than for the one who was fortunate enough to experience basic trust as an infant. However, everyone has a powerful inner resource to call upon. All challenges in upbringing can be overcome. Our true nature is unlimited.

SILENCE

A social stigma is sometimes attached to the intentional experience of silence. It is ridiculed as navel-gazing. It seems opposed to the values of exerting oneself or seeking to add to one's knowledge of the world. It is considered by some as a waste of time or as an exercise in self-deception. On the other hand, it has become acceptable as a form of relaxation and stress-reduction.

Our experience of life has an outer and an inner aspect. Outwardly, we observe the world and interact with it. Inwardly, we have our private thoughts, feelings, and sensations. Thoughtfulness and reflection are deeper inner experiences. And still deeper we find love, compassion, insight, inspiration, and creativity. We don't know where these feelings and knowings come from. They seem to be spontaneous gifts that well up from inside. Entering the silence is more than a practice of stress-reduction. It means plumbing the depths of the inner world. It means developing an untapped capacity. The inner world might seem like a place of emptiness, a void; but it is a potent void, the source of a wealth of spontaneous knowings and feelings.

To find the rare gems glimmering in Rumi's metaphoric basement, we have to tear down the house. The social construct we call our self, the ego, is intoxicated with the endless fascination of life's experiences. Those experiences are speaking to us of a deeper meaning, but we have trouble seeing it because our perspective is too narrow. Tearing down the house means doubting that our presumed self is the truth about who we are. There is a larger story we have been missing. When we come to know the inner life, we will find that it broadens our view of our self and the world. We will become sobered and take life's ups and downs more calmly. We will discover meaning and purpose to be everywhere and will begin to see our part in it.

It is not necessarily easy to enter the silence. Our minds are hyperactive, and we are accustomed to paying attention to their chatter. Most of us can't turn it off. Even worse, as soon as we cut ourselves off from the constant distractions of our daily lives, the undigested material of the psyche bobs to the surface, seeking our attention. From our usual vantage point, we gauge our unresolved issues according to our judgment of ourselves. We feel deceived, betrayed, and abused; or inadequate, unlovable, and trapped, because of our habitual way of perceiving our self. But this is just what we have been trying to escape by feeding our minds a steady diet of distractions. We discover first that the mind is unruly, and then find that the heart is unruly too. Diving into the silence then might become associated with unpleasant thoughts and feelings.

Another hazard could arise: a fear of losing oneself, of being carried off into a disorienting state of nothingness—a survival fear. We are accustomed to our socially constructed sense of self. If we begin to doubt it and enter a state of suspension of our usual assumptions, if we fall out of our narrowness into an expanded state, we might get dizzy or disoriented. We might feel as though we are falling without a sense of up or down or where we might land. We need to find new ground to support us. Our usual sense of identity has given us at least a familiar sense of orientation. We know where we stand, and can relate and react from that place. This sense of falling, of not being able to find solid ground under our feet was captured well by the poet Rainer Maria Rilke in the poem "Autumn."

> *The leaves are falling, falling as if from far up,*
> *as if orchards were dying high in space.*
> *Each leaf falls as if it were motioning "no."*
> *And tonight the heavy earth is falling*
> *away from all other stars in the loneliness.*
> *We're all falling. This hand here is falling.*
> *And look at the other one. It's in them all.*
> *And yet there is Someone, whose hands*
> *infinitely calm, holding up all this falling.*[1]

Rilke is pointing to an intuition that arises in this state of losing one's familiar identity. We are floating, uncertain of who we are; and yet there seems to be something supporting us. That mysterious wellspring, which has been supplying us with spontaneous thoughts and feelings all along, now becomes more apparent. We are afloat in a continual creative flow. We are no longer so predictable. Each moment is a new gift, fresh and novel. However, this comforting intuition may not come at once.

Confronting the obstacles previously mentioned, one might turn away from silence thinking this is not for me. But what a loss. The wealth that silence holds is available to everyone. Accessing it takes some patience and practice.

---

1 Rainer Maria Rilke, *The Winged Energy of Delight: Selected Translations*, Trans. Robert Bly (New York: Harper Perennial, 2005).

ENTERING THE SILENCE

WHAT happens when you close your eyes in a quiet place and intentionally enter the silence? First, your senses may become heightened. You hear sounds more keenly and feel the air on your skin. You might feel your heart beating or be aware of other sensations in the body. You might have the sensation of floating. If you ease your breathing, you may become deeply relaxed. You may have a sensation of diffuse light. Perhaps some images may float through your mind. Pretty soon thoughts appear as memory flashes or reminders of things to do or impressions of the day. Perhaps a scene or a face appears. Images may come and go quickly.

If anything is bothering you, you will probably first feel it as stress in your stomach or back or neck or face. You can counter the stress by noticing it, and then relaxing the part of the body that holds it. If something comes up that you want to remember, you can jot it down and set it aside for later. If an unresolved feeling comes up—guilt or resentment or self-judgment—you could write it down or choose to examine it as it comes up. By confronting such feelings in the moment, trying to relax the tension around them, trying to observe them non-judgmentally, as though listening compassionately to a friend, you may make progress in loosening the grip the feelings have on you.

If you decide to put aside whatever comes, there is a way to become more proactive about entering the silence. You might think that you must become passive to experience silence. This puts you at the mercy of thoughts and feelings that are clamoring for attention. I have found that entering the silence is easier if I use a simple concentration. Breathing out, I imagine I am filling my inner visual field with light. Breathing in, I imagine simply resting in a field of light. After doing this for a short time, I find that my experience of silence is peaceful and pleasant. It feels restful and renewing. You can also try the same kind of concentration on the breath imagining a field of love. Breathing out, you radiate love and breathing in, you feel immersed in a field of love.

If you can fully relax, you might have a feeling of suspension. Nothing seems to be happening. More subtly, you might perceive a feeling of settling, as though the stimulation of ordinary consciousness is winding down, like snowflakes settling in a snow globe that was turned over. If it is quiet enough, you might notice the sound of silence: a continual subtle ringing in the ears. Once you have found this inner sound, you can use it like a beacon to carry you into the silence. Though it resembles a sound, it belongs to the silence.

Impatience could set in. When will something happen? We hardly notice the restlessness and agitation that attends our overstimulated contemporary lifestyle. When we try to be still, what may become apparent is a feeling of impatience. There is a subtle pressure to get to the next thing that robs us of enjoying the experience of the moment.

The Sufi master Hazrat Inayat Khan walked with a slow and stately gait. It was the walk of a king, never rushed. What happens if you try to walk as though you had all the time in the world, with each step enjoying the world around you? Can you feel the impatience that propels you forward to the next appointment or goal? Can you let go of that pressure and be present in the moment?

When you enter the silence, see if you can notice that same pressure disturbing your peace. You can practice becoming more aware of restlessness in daily life. You can learn step by step to let it go and experience patience as a relief rather than a burden.

Entering the silence can be like taking a brief retreat from the world. You can set aside all worries, obligations, and responsibilities. You can enjoy some moments of freedom. When you give yourself time to be still, your body, mind, and psyche automatically restore themselves. The process is similar to deep sleep. When we withdraw from the world and shut down all the ways we try to control our lives, we give a natural restorative process a chance to bring our many complex homeostatic systems back into balance. That produces a feeling of peace and well-being.

It may be that there is a threshold you have to cross before you are able to sink into the silence. When I first tried to sit still, I found my body to be quite restless. Here is a practice that helped me settle my body: I challenged myself to sit still without moving a muscle for twenty minutes. Sometime toward the end of those twenty minutes, my body became peaceful. I never had to repeat that exercise. After that, I was always able to sit still.

Becoming comfortable in the silence not only gives the nervous system a rest, but it also opens up the inner senses. Learning how to enter the inner world establishes communication with the pure intelligence that is the essence of who you are. It is the source of intuition. Most of us are used to making decisions or resolving problems by thinking things through. We use a rational process that weighs pros and cons, and we hope to find the best solution. Those who are fortunate to have a strong intuition rely on a feeling, a hunch for guidance. When you become used to entering the silence, suspending your rational faculties and relaxing deeply, you can pose a question and you will find that unexpected insights will come; guidance will open doors and make sense of your life. The Sufi mystics call this experience *contemplation*.

You might think of cultivating silence and stillness as a key that lets you into the treasury of inner resources — insight, inspiration, and creativity. In the beginning, it is enough to find a place of respite. If entering the silence can become a habit, a place of repose to balance the incessant activity of our lives, then, over time, the inner life will gradually reveal its treasures.

Making friends with the silence is a skill you can call on later in the adventure of finding meaning and purpose.

FACING THE DRAGON

WHEN you wish to enter the inner life, to cultivate silence, to tap intuition, and find the treasures of meaning hidden there, you first encounter the ceaseless chatter of subvocal thoughts, sometimes called *monkey mind*. At a deeper level, you are assailed by disturbing feelings. The enduring fascination of Robert Lewis Stevenson's Dr. Jekyl and Mr. Hyde is the mesmerizing horror of witnessing the struggle between our good and evil inclinations. Freud shed light on this turmoil in the psyche by framing it as a battle between the id and the superego, with the ego acting as the manager trying to function in life while keeping the struggle private. Jung went further by identifying the shadow side of the psyche: those rejected parts of ourselves that we split off and relegate to the subconscious.

In many spiritual traditions, the struggle with the ego plays a central role. In contrast to the meaning Freud gave to the ego, in this case *ego* means the sense of a separate self: the false or limited self. By separating itself from the wholeness or seamlessness of reality, the ego acquires its negative tendencies: selfishness, greed, jealousy, resentment, hatred, and cruelty.

Some of the ego's demons may have become lost to view by splitting off. Naturally, we have developed a resistance to looking at these aspects of ourselves. We project our negative feelings on to others. By judging and criticizing others, we may develop a cynical view of our fellow humans and a self-pitying attitude toward ourselves as victims of injustice. We rationalize those faults we recognize, make excuses for them, or surrender to them when we say, "That's just who I am." Meanwhile we suffer from guilt, shame, and depression when we judge ourselves harshly.

Rather than settle for a standoff and a feeling of precarious self-esteem, we can choose to meet our shortcomings head on. One way to approach the inner struggle is to disidentify with the limited self: see it as an instrument that has been given to us to serve our purpose. It is our job to train the stubborn ego, brother donkey. By being clear about your values, about the ideal you would like to live up to, you can catch sibling donkey falling beneath the ideal and exercise your will to learn the lesson and not repeat the behavior. Chastising the limited self or sinking into remorse and depression doesn't help. Use all the energy at your disposal to strengthen the commitment to do better. Each time you succeed in doing what feels right, celebrate the victory.

Another way to proceed is radical acceptance. It comes from recognizing that we are not here to be angels but rather to be human in its best sense. We have all tendencies in us, from the laudable to the most heinous. Thich Nhat Hanh expressed this beautifully in his poem "Call Me by My True Names."

> *I am the child in Uganda, all skin and bones,*
> *my legs as thin as bamboo sticks,*
> *and I am the arms merchant,*
> *selling deadly weapons to Uganda.*

and I am the pirate,
my heart not yet capable of seeing and loving.

Once we accept that, like everyone, we are capable of all feelings and acts, we can accept those parts of ourself that we would rather deny. We acknowledge that what we have rejected is indeed part of us. It doesn't mean that we give in to those parts of our self that we reject. We accept responsibility to control those feelings and to sublimate their impetus into something desirable. As Thich Nhat Hanh says, we open our heart and trust its impulse when it is vulnerable and loving.

Please call me by my true names,
so I can wake up,
and so the door of my heart can be left open,
the door of compassion.[1]

The Sufis have a name for this process: *muhasabah* or *examination of conscience*. We have an inherent knowledge of what is right and wrong. Our conscience keeps track of whether or not we listen to that innate knowing. If we make a habit of consulting our conscience, learning from its counsel, and acting to make amends for whatever it tells us we have done wrong, we lift a heavy psychic load off our shoulders. We can walk with a lighter step. Our conscience is clear.

The inner struggle to lift ourselves out of the pit of separateness and isolation, the burden of the limited self, is a lifelong effort. However, as we become more self-aware, as we gain a sense of dignity in living closer to our ideals; as we clear away the debris that obscures our inner self, the struggle becomes easier and our

1   Thich Nhat Hanh, *Call Me by My True Names* (Berkeley, CA: Parallax Press, 1999), 72.

ability to control the little self grows. The barrier that separates us from the treasure of the inner life thins, and our path in life's journey opens up.

How can you go about examining your conscience? There are three questions you can reflect upon. First, *have you done something that has hurt or wronged another?* It may have been done in the heat of emotion. It could have happened as a reflexive reaction that leaped out of you before you had a chance to consider it. On the other hand, you may have done something intentionally, which you felt was right at the time but, upon reflection, you have come to regret. Perhaps subsequently it bothered you, but you found a way to justify it, or you brushed it off as inconsequential or water under the bridge. But it has continued to nag at you. The irritation corrodes your self-respect and disturbs your peace.

What can you do about it now? Can you humble yourself and ask for forgiveness even if you think the other person has forgotten it, or will react with hostility? Do you need to offer to do something to make amends for past mistakes? The price you pay may be painful for the ego, but the reward is renewed self-respect and a settled peaceful feeling. You can breathe more freely and your burden is eased.

The second question to consider is, *am I holding on to any resentments?* Is there anyone I have been holding a grudge against, and am I now ready to forgive? We begin life with an open heart. Wounded over and over again, we become tough, covering over our vulnerability and, at the same time, closing down the heart. But what is life without love? Bitterness is sustained by nursing resentments, holding grudges, or clinging to hatred. Though harsh feelings may well be justified by callous abuse or cruel betrayal, yet you are punishing yourself by allowing such feelings to harden the heart.

If you are not ready to forgive, then you can be compassionate and patient, and not add to your burden by judging yourself.

When the time is right, you can proceed by trying to look at the offense through the eyes of the offender. Why did that person do what they did? If you can imagine seeing the situation from the other person's point of view, you may gain some insight. Once you understand the other person, it becomes easier to forgive. We are all human; we all make mistakes. There are reasons why we act the way we do. When we can forgive ourselves and forgive others, our hearts can again open and we can feel once again our capacity for love.

And then there is the third question, *am I holding a grudge against my fate?* Do I feel that, somehow, life is against me? Have I elevated my particular limitations as proof that while others have found their niche, I am adrift in life? Everyone's limitations seem to be tailored for one's unique challenges. By meeting those challenges, you can grow and discover your gifts. If your attitude is resentful, seeing that you are hampered while others seem to have adapted, then you are holding yourself back. Can you welcome and appreciate your handicaps?

As long as you feel that you have been shortchanged, you handicap yourself. Instead of feeling angry and bitter about your fate, dissolve those feelings by remembering all the blessings you have received in life, especially all those blessings that come every day and which we mostly take for granted.

The story of the transformation of Scrooge in Dickens's *A Christmas Carol*, shows how a man hardened by greed and embittered by denying his heart's wish in his youth, woke up and realized that he could still find beauty and love in life by caring for others. His delight and exuberance upon waking on Christmas morning is a sign of the promise that examining the conscience holds out to us.

The trait that fulfills what it means to be human is compassion. We are capable of imagining perfection, and we suffer when we fall beneath that ideal. Knowing that everyone struggles with faults and regrets, when the heart is warm, we can understand and forgive. But if we are preoccupied with our own "sins," the heart will remain frozen. How hard it is to forgive ourselves. A religious person receives forgiveness from an unconditionally loving God. If you don't have that kind of faith, you could imagine stepping out away from your limited self. Can you adopt the perspective of the Witness, the intelligence that looks out through your eyes? Can you look at yourself as though viewing another person? It is easier to see another person with compassion and forgive that person for the same behavior that you would condemn in yourself. Imagine that you, as the Witness, are a kind parent observing yourself as your child. You see the mistakes but also the underlying purity and the future promise. If you can find a way to forgive yourself and clean the slate, you can melt your heart and more easily forgive others.

our own ideal

→ forgive you — will be forgiven

& vice-versa

35

INNATE PERFECTION

WHAT motivates us? We strive to reach something better, to better ourselves, or conditions for ourselves or for those we care about. We have the ability to imagine an improvement. What is more mysterious is that we have an innate ability to imagine perfection. Where can we see perfection in the world? Wherever there is excellence we can also find some limitation, some imperfection. It is the nature of this world that we can approach perfection, but true perfection will always elude us.

Then why did Jesus say, "Be ye therefore perfect, even as your Father which is in heaven is perfect"?[1] Those who have a religious faith identify their conception of perfection as God. How can one become as perfect as God or as one's ideal vision of perfection?

Try as we might, although we can imagine that there is such a thing as perfection, our mind falters when trying to capture it. It is beyond the power of the mind. Yet we can have an intimation of perfection through our feelings.

Choose a quality that you admire. For example, imagine the quality of honesty. Then imagine a more perfect honesty. With each breath put your whole heart into envisioning the fullness of honesty. Images of

1 Matthew 5:48.

honest individuals or acts of honesty may flit through your mind. You may become charmed by the thought of a pristine honesty. At some point, you may feel as though you are crossing a threshold. Instead of exerting your imagination to hold a vision of honesty, you find yourself absorbed in its atmosphere. You are drawn in, attracted to it. The quality you choose to imagine reveals itself to you.

Perfection is self-revealing. We perceive it in an exalted state. Then we discover that it belongs to us. To claim it, we need to value it and to seek it ardently. It does not disclose itself to the casually curious, only to its lover.

I believe that when Jesus said, "Be ye perfect," he meant to encourage us to reclaim the self-revealing perfection that is not only available for us to experience, but which we can discover as our true nature. Our essence, the *I* that looks out through our eyes, is the true nature that Jesus urged us to recognize. When we remember who we are, pure intelligence or spirit, we find perfection in our inner life. That perfection can help navigate our lives in the outer world of limitation.

What influence does the impression of perfection have on our lives? Once we have tasted the exaltation of perfection, we will look for ways to bring it into our everyday lives and our strivings. If we make it into a self-improvement project, we will soon come up against our limitations and become mired in the frustration of perfectionism. Instead, we need to relax, open up, and trust that our true nature is perfection. Then perfection will flow into our activities as a gift freely given.

Perfection cannot be distinguished by itself. To be recognized for what it is, perfection needs limitation to provide a contrast. The Sufis say that the universal intelligence is able to know its perfection by comparing it with our limitation. Thus our imperfections serve a useful purpose. We may be able to endure them more easily if we think of them as a gift we can offer to the process of the unseen coming to know itself.

Awakening to meaning and our purpose, and taking up the challenge of actualizing it, calls upon and brings out our innate sense of perfection.

Working with Perfection

WHAT is keeping us from discovering a sense of perfection, trusting it, and being inspired by it? We are impressed with our limitations. We are continually confronted with our shortcomings, with the restrictions imposed by conditions, and with an awareness of the dire situations surrounding us, locally and worldwide. We are imprisoned by intangible chains. Our minds hold firmly a conviction of our smallness and feebleness in the face of staggering challenges.

How can we believe that perfection is our true nature, when imperfection is constantly before our eyes, mocking the visions of our sensitive inner life? First, we need to free ourselves from the emotional grip that our sense of limitation holds us in. Can we step back and take a more detached view of ourselves and the world? Can we step out of our narrow point of view into a wider vision?

Our condition is like the boy raised by peasants, who was hired at the castle of the king to perform a humble task. He was gradually promoted and given greater and greater responsibilities. As he succeeded and grew in confidence and rose to a position of great honor, one day he was brought before the king, who revealed to him that he was the king's beloved son who had been lost as an infant. The king had found him and gradually reconciled him with his princely state.

Our outer condition of limitation has blinded us to our true nature, which has great power and nobility. For most of us, the revelation of who we are has to come little by little. We are not ready to grasp the nature of our inner life all at once. Like the peasant prince, we have to learn about it gradually.

What is most important is the changing of the point of view. Shift the focus of your attention off your presumed self. See whatever is happening as the perfection of the universal intelligence trying to express itself and discover itself through the imperfect instrument you have become accustomed to calling yourself. Side with the greater self. You are the one empowered to do something about the difficulty perfection encounters when trying to express itself through the resistance of matter. When things go wrong, focus your attention on what is trying to come through, and use your creative imagination and will power to do what you can to facilitate that passage. Be compassionate toward brother donkey, while at the same time pressing that donkey to excel.

The awareness of our limitations needn't bring us down. See it as an opportunity to learn and grow. We can bring our behavior and our personality more in line with our ideal of perfection, step by step, by noting our limitations and trying to do better.

Similarly, seeing the world as a place of limitation, we can take the crises and challenges we see around us as opportunities to do better. Although the situation in the world looks grim, a case could be made that there has been a general improvement historically in the degree of justice, well-being, and human behavior in the world.

Can you view the limitations in yourself and the crises in the world as works in progress, as challenges designed to bring forth a little further the latent perfection that is the catalyst of all our motivations? Can we begin the work of freeing ourselves from our obsession with shortcomings and insoluble problems, and shift our attention to the inexhaustible resource of perfection, the stuff we are made from?

The journey of finding and pursuing one's purpose in life, leads to the gradual realization of the perfection of the inner life and its guidance toward reconciling ourselves with our true nature.

THE NATURE OF UNITY

WHAT is the nature of unity? The perspective we are used to is multiplicity, the abundance of forms. Our mind thinks in opposites: light and dark, good and bad, hot and cold. We give things names to distinguish them from one another. How can we imagine a state of unity, where nothing can be distinguished from anything else with our dualistic minds?

Can we perceive unity with the heart instead of the mind? We seek closeness in our most intimate relationships. Loving another brings us closer to that other. We have a desire to unite or merge with the other. If our heart's reach expands, we feel kinship with family, friends, community, nation; perhaps also with nature. We recognize a shared magnetism of life running through all things, a common vitality. We intuit an essential current we might call *spirit*. It doesn't seem to be material. It is a mystery. We can't test its validity in a repeatable experiment. It is an insight of the heart.

Our inquiring minds would like to identify this spirit, pin it down, know about it by grasping its properties. But as we just saw, we are used to thinking dualistically. We know something by comparing it with something else. But the nature of unity is that it cannot be grasped by the inquiring mind. There is nothing it can be compared to, because it encompasses all. There is nothing outside of it, nothing aside from it.

We are drawn to unity in other ways. We wish for harmony and cooperation among nations. Physicists seek a grand unification theory. In sports we sometimes speak jokingly of becoming one with a bat or a golf club or a tennis racket. Concentration in sports helps one to forget oneself. Undivided attention brings a unity of focus that maximizes the athlete's responsiveness. Artists also experience losing themselves by becoming absorbed in their work. When you forget yourself while pouring your attention into a task you love, something else seems to take over. There is a loss of separation. Some have described it as entering a flow. The flow seems to be an outpouring of inspiration that comes from beyond the mind and beyond the individual.

This suggests that our sense of individuality keeps us from experiencing a state of unity. When we forget ourselves because we are moved or inspired or transfixed, a door opens to a source of life and renewal that seems to lie beyond the perceived world of the senses. How does our individuality blind us to an underlying unity that is life-giving and inspiring?

Our sense of limitation blinds us to the state of perfection that already exists in our inner life. But further, our presumed self is threatened by the idea of losing itself. We don't mind when we are carried away in moments of exaltation. But deliberately putting oneself aside is another matter. We are attached to the social construct that we construe as our self. And we fear that without our usual identity we would be lost in a netherworld.

The drama of the limited self and true self has been explored through the imagination of the heart by Sufi mystics. They picture it as the relationship of the lover and the Beloved. Through grace, the lover has been given a glimpse of the perfect Beloved, the One who loves unconditionally. Those who have had a near-death experience tell of an encounter with a being of light who knows you intimately, and who radiates unconditional love. They report feeling so safe and so thoroughly seen and embraced, that they lose their fear of death and prefer not to return to life. This is the state of the lover in life. After once having been smitten by the perfume of the Beloved's presence, the lover feels the pain of separation and longs continually for union with the Beloved. The Sufi poet Rumi says, "The Beloved is all in all, the lover only veils Him; the Beloved is all that lives, the lover a dead thing."[1] Like the artist, the lover forgets himself or herself because love keeps the focus on the vision of the Beloved.

But the Sufis have taken this relationship further by looking at it from the Beloved's point of view. The Beloved represents the state of perfection and unity. In a state of unity, the Beloved cannot know itself. There are no boundaries, nothing that would allow discrimination of one aspect from another. The Beloved depends upon the world of duality to discover its nature. Without a world of limitation, there would be no opportunity to have a relationship; there would be no chance to express and receive love. While the lover wishes for union with the Beloved, the Beloved wishes for separation in order to experience love. Out of regard for the wish of the Beloved, the lover makes the sacrifice of accepting the pain of separation. Our life in this world entails a sacrifice, living in this world of limitation and loss. Pursuing the purpose of your life is a love gift to the Beloved to whom you belong.

Where is this Beloved to be found?

---

1 Jelaluddin Rumi, *The Masnavi,* book I, trans. E.H. Whinfield (London: 1898).

We can see unity in the functioning of the body. The body consists of many parts. We receive a multitude of sensations. Yet somehow we integrate all the parts into a sense of self, a unified whole. If we hit our thumb with a hammer, our whole self experiences the pain as well as the thumb. We don't have to consciously coordinate the many parts to perform an action. It all functions as an integrated whole.

We might also have a sense of unity as a family or ethnicity or gender or community or nation. If we ever encountered aliens, we might unite as human beings. These unities are always defined by an in- and an out-group. But suppose your identity extended so far that everything was included in the in-group. Then in the words of the Sufis, everywhere you turn you would see the face of the One.[2]

There are other metaphors for the condition of unity that underlie the apparent world of multiplicity. The discovery of the interdependence of living systems upon each other, called *ecology*, has been further elaborated in Chaos Theory. The example of a butterfly, flapping its wings in one part of the world, triggering a storm thousands of miles away illustrates the interconnectedness of a super-sensitive network. The condition of unity can be pictured as a network that connects everything to everything else. It is not only a physical network, but one that links everything psychically. Every thought and feeling radiates out through the network and has its effect on everything else.

The Gaia hypothesis suggests that the planet like a person has a way of functioning as a coordinated whole. Gaia is imagined as a kind of integrated organism. Now suppose that everything we can imagine, the entire universe of matter, energy, thought, feeling, and

---

2 Qur'an 2:115.

45

consciousness also functions as an integrated organism. This is another way to conceive of the condition of unity.

If you struggle with the concept of unity, trying to understand how there could be a relationship between the All and an individual, or how there could be unity and separation at the same time, your mind will strike the wall of enigma and paradox. To make use of this wisdom, you have to rely on the sensitivity of a loving heart. If you are willing to let your mind be blown, and open your heart to the possibility of unconditional love and the peace and stillness of unity, how is this of any use in finding and living your life's purpose?

Jesus advised us, "Seek ye first the kingdom of God and His righteousness, and all these things shall be added to you."[3] The power and inspiration we need to accomplish our purpose can best be found in seeking our own source.

---

3 Matthew 6:33.

Implications of Unity

WHAT are the implications of viewing fundamental reality as a state of unity? If we suppose for a moment that duality or multiplicity is apparent to our senses but illusory, and the true underlying reality is unity, then the appearance of a multitude of sentient beings must resolve itself into one single being that experiences itself in a multitude of ways. One intelligence peers out through a multitude of eyes and other senses. Our true self is the only being, the one single self; and our presumed self is a medium through which the one self is discovering itself.

Unity also implies wholeness, an integration of a multitude of parts. Everything is interconnected and interdependent. We tend to lack this feeling as individuals. We are aware of isolation and loneliness. We feel we are missing something. When we recover from illness we might say that we feel whole again. A healthy body is one in which all the parts are coordinated and working smoothly. You may have had the experience of falling in love and finding in your partner what you felt was missing in yourself. You find in the relationship a sense of wholeness, a puzzle whose parts fit neatly together.

Our surface identity is indeed missing much. Intuitively, we know that we are meant to be more than we seem to be. We suffer from feeling a lack of wholeness, which is like a chronic illness. The discovery of unity as our true source and fountainhead, is the healthy wholeness we are seeking, the recovery from what seemed to be incurable. On the surface, we have only sprouted a tentative budding; while at our roots, in potential, lies a wealth of trunk, branch, leaf, flower, and fruit. Everything is within us in the depth.

Unity is also seamless. There are no boundaries in a unitary reality. In duality, the parts are distinguished by boundaries. If duality is an illusion, a superficial appearance of things, then apparent boundaries are illusory. The sun in the sky seems to have a well-defined boundary to our eyes, but the light from the sun proceeds out into space. The earth and all of the planets in the solar system are immersed in it. There is no boundary between the solar disk that we see and the light that flows out into space. Our bodies seem to be bounded by our skin, but our bodies radiate heat: infrared radiation that has no definite boundary, and which merges with the radiant heat of our surroundings. We are taking in oxygen, circulating it through our respiratory and circulatory systems, where it touches every cell and then returns as carbon dioxide to the environment. We ingest mineral, plant, and animal life, and return the remains to the earth.

There is evidence that our consciousness has no definite boundary. Mothers who are bonded to their children, in time of war sometimes know when their child has been injured or killed in battle. Many have had the experience of anticipating the caller before picking up an unexpected phone call. Psychic knowings are commonplace. We find that we can sometimes accurately read the mind of another.

As the heart softens and opens, the illusory dualistic boundaries between us fade. Compassion and affection link us to others. Gradually our network of caring expands, and we catch a glimpse of the unity of the human family. With the dawning of a vision of unity on our horizon, we develop a taste for serving others.

We function as though we are separate entities with privacy and loneliness. If unity is the underlying reality, our individual and collective health lies in wholeness, and we are seamlessly connected to all other beings.

Sounding Your Note

ARE you not a unique individual? Is there anyone else among billions on the planet who is just like you?

As we grow and mature through adolescence, we learn by imitation from the models we admire. We seek to find ourselves by adopting a variety of persona. Eventually we settle on an identity that works for us. As we age, we value becoming more authentic, discarding old masks.

The Sufi mystic Pir Vilayat Inayat Khan said, "Dare to have the courage to be who you could be if you would be who you should be." (Later he replaced the "should" with "could" because he didn't want to encourage anyone to "should" themselves.) I believe the meaning he intended is that we have an innate and noble nature, and all that stands in the way of living it is a lack of courage and will to step into it.

We each have a note to sound in the symphony of the whole. The metaphor of a symphony conveys the idea of the harmonious working of an interconnected whole. By sounding our note, we take part in the vast ecological network of aspiring souls, which resonates subliminally like a symphony of surpassing beauty.

The Sufi poet Sa'adi once said, "Every soul is meant for a certain purpose, and the light of that purpose has been kindled in that soul."[1] The light of our purpose has been kindled in our soul. It may remain unconscious. Nevertheless it is kindled. When you wake up to the purpose of your life, you begin to sound your note. And if you don't sound your note, the symphony of the whole is incomplete. It is our privilege and our satisfaction in life to sound our note.

How do you find out what note is yours to sound? By paying attention. If you notice what gives you pleasure, what inspires you, and what gives you a sense of peace and satisfaction, then it seems as if everything is speaking to you, telling you about your note and your purpose. Those things that inspire you or otherwise speak to you are trying to tell you about your note.

Besides paying attention, reflecting on what you observe will also help. Take time to hold before your mind the clues you have noticed in a quiet, peaceful state. If you have practiced relaxing into silence, this will help you resist analysis. Suspension of outer knowledge and mental effort, and entrance into the fecund state of a peaceful inner life will bring clarity and fresh insights from the clues you hold before you.

Sounding your note may mean daring to be who you really are. It may mean becoming the person you would like to be. Or it may mean finding the path or goal in life that brings meaning and satisfaction, actively making a vision into a reality. Or it may mean both. You may be drawn to shape your personality to better reflect your ideal, making your life into a work of art. Or you may wish to shape the materials of the world to build something or express something. You may be moved by the needs of others to devote your life

---

1 Hazrat Inayat Khan, "Esoteric Papers: The Gathas" (Unpublished).

to service. No goal is any better than any other. Your note is the right note for you.

Muppet puppeteer Jim Henson knew from an early age that he had a unique note to sound. In the book *Imagine*, Henson speaks about calling and guidance.

> I believe in taking a positive attitude toward the world, toward people, and toward my work. I think I'm here for a purpose. I think it's likely that we all are, but I'm only sure about myself. I try to tune myself in to whatever it is that I'm supposed to be, and I try to think of myself as a part of all of us—all mankind and all life. I find it's not easy to keep these lofty thoughts in mind as the day goes by, but it certainly helps me a great deal to start out this way. . . .
>
> I don't know exactly where ideas come from, but when I'm working well ideas just appear. I've heard other people say similar things—so it's one of the ways I know there's help and guidance out there. It's just a matter of our figuring out how to receive the ideas or information that's there waiting to be heard.[2]

Every musician who plays with others, or singer who sings in a group, knows those moments when the parts blend together, when the harmonies mesh. The difference between being slightly off and moving into sync is like two different worlds. Magic happens. The gates of heaven open up.

Sounding one's note is meshing with cosmic harmony. It brings elation, happiness, and peace.

---

2 *Imagine*, edited and compiled by Gina Misiroglu (Novato, CA: New World Library, 1999), 24.

SPIRIT INVOLUTION

WHAT is evident to our senses is the world of matter. Nature presents to our senses a fascinating and intricate network of relationships, and the questions that science allows us to ask have resulted in an explosion of knowledge about our world. The science of evolution has explained much about how complex organic forms have arisen from simple origins. Cosmology has revealed the origins of the large features of the cosmos, and has pushed back our understanding of the origin of matter and energy to the frontiers of the Big Bang.

But what if what we are coming to understand is actually the evolution of the innumerable instruments of intelligence or consciousness or spirit? Is there another story that runs parallel to the evolution we observe in matter? According to the insights of mystic traditions, the other story is the involution of spirit.

Consider the metaphysical metaphor for creation that derives from a Hadith Qudsi, a saying of Prophet Muhammad that is ascribed to God speaking through him. "I was a Hidden Treasure and I longed to be known, so I created the world that I might know Myself." Imagine the Only Being, a perfect intelligence in a state of utter unity. The Only Being cannot know itself because there are no parts to comprehend. It is one unique seamless thing. In order to know itself, it creates a cosmos out of itself. In the beginning the cosmos still has little differentiation. Furthermore, what emerges initially has little capacity for intelligence to function.

Probing the mystery of the fundamental nature of matter, science has encountered behavior on the smallest scales that remains baffling. On that scale, matter retains a condition of indeterminacy; it can't be pinned down. Its behavior seems to depend on how it is observed, as though, being part of the seamless network, we cannot remove ourselves as observers. String Theory, albeit a mathematical speculation, seems to suggest that vibration is the most fundamental property of matter. Mystics describe the earliest state of creation as vibration. Could matter be condensed spirit as some mystics claim?

Imagine pure intelligence condensing into a primal form of matter. Over eons, matter takes on forms that are capable of evolution. Spirit gradually works its way through grades of consciousness in matter, making its way toward self-awareness. There is a saying of a Sufi dervish: "God slept in the rock, dreamt in the plant, awoke in the animal and became fully conscious in man."[1]

Is this idea another version of Intelligent Design? Not exactly. Involution is the process by which intelligence emerges more and more, in ever more perceptive and sophisticated instruments. Involution of spirit does not present an alternative to natural selection. It does not posit an external, supernatural control that directs evolution. Rather it pictures the underlying driving forces of nature, like the desire to live, the desire to reproduce, and the desire to know, as fundamental properties of

---

1 Hazrat Inayat Khan, *The Sufi Message* (London: Barrie and Rockliff, 1963), 5: 252.

spirit and, therefore, of matter, which takes its existence from spirit. Without a desire to live and to reproduce, how could natural selection function?

Spirit is not imagined as an external God, imprinting its plan on nature and on the course of evolution, but rather spirit is seen as the underlying nature of matter, which is evolving toward more and more conscious forms because of the desire to know. The outcome may not be predetermined, but may rather be continually adapting to circumstances through the creative faculty of nature itself, stemming from its primal condition as pure intelligence.

From this perspective, our body, mind, and heart are gifts from eons of evolutionary horticulture. We are the recipients of prize instruments tested in the crucible of selection's fire, with keenly honed sensitivity. We are the only type of instrument we know of that is capable of self-awareness. And that self-awareness can be put in the service of the unfolding spirit. At last spirit can awaken to its own nature.

And so it appears that our life, our desires, and our nature are deeply rooted in the emergence and awakening of spirit. If our reaction is that spirit is something alien that threatens to take us over, this would be a very disturbing idea.

Recall that we left off an earlier exploration of the question, *Who am I?*, postponing the next step for later. Now we take up this question again. At that point, we imagined the pure intelligence that peers through my eyes and the eyes of others, as being a sense of self that persists, which has been with us throughout our life. It is the bare sense of *I* that is left when all the attributes that are constantly changing are stripped away. Now identify spirit as your experience of the basic sense of *I*, the observer or witness watching all objectively. The spirit that wishes to know itself is your deepest sense of yourself.

Can you feel a shift happening when you see yourself and your life as the phenomenon of a universal spirit, a pure intelligence, emerging gently out of its cocoon, to discover ineffable beauty? In a different metaphor, can you see your dreams and desires as the stirring of seeds, so that a plant can push up into the sunlight and produce an exquisite flower?

The mystic would say that you can attune yourself to the infinite. Picture your identity as a string, one end of which is fixed to your limited self and the other end extending to infinity. By reminding ourselves that our consciousness can reach out to a state that is perfect and unlimited, we can slowly shift our perception of reality.

Intelligence

So far I have suggested that everyone is capable of an intuitive impression of intelligence when imagining the barest sense of yourself, the sense of *I*. Let's examine further what I mean by intelligence. When we speak of intelligence, we usually mean relative intelligence: Mary is more intelligent than Jack, or this plan is more intelligent than the others. But while we can discriminate a greater or lesser intelligence, we can never say what intelligence is in itself. And yet we have no trouble recognizing intelligence in itself. When the mind stops trying to define intelligence, what it is becomes apparent. We have an immediate recognition of intelligence. And as intelligent creatures, we become aware that intelligence is our basic or root nature. Individual intelligence is particular, but basic intelligence is universal. The same intelligence I find to be my essence, is no different than the intelligence anyone else would find to be their essence. It can't be quantified. What makes it greater or lesser in the individual is the capacity of the instrument to contain it and express it. The intelligence that is available to every one of us is unlimited.

Do we anthropomorphize intelligence? Is the unlimited intelligence a human intelligence? It is the same animating spirit that breathes life into not only every human but every plant and animal and supplies the magnetism of every inanimate object. To say that it is a human intelligence would limit it. Rather, we could say that comprehension of our own intelligence gives a clue to the nature of the primal intelligence.

Throughout this book, we return again and again to the principle of forgetting the limited self in order to awaken to the unlimited self. The Sufis even speak of annihilating the false ego in the real. I have put forward the idea that the self-concept is a socially constructed fiction and therefore not real.

I have personally found it valuable to question the reality of my self-concept, to relax my concern about it, and to observe it more objectively. But here I would like to revisit ideas about ego and self-concept, which can be taken too simplistically. While the self-concept is constructed by impressions one has received from others, it does reflect inheritances passed down from parents and ancestors. Also, as anyone who has spent time observing a new-born will agree, the infant arrives with a distinctive personality, and not all traits can be traced to family genetics. Every individual is unique. From the spiritual point of view, spirit wishes to know itself in each individual in a unique way, and disposes the infant with certain qualities whose combination has never before existed and will never exist again. The impressions from others that shape our self-concept stem from these earthly and spiritual inheritances. So although the self-concept is not real, it is a reflection of something that is real.

When the Sufis or mystics of other paths speak of annihilating the ego, they don't necessarily mean destroying the self-concept, but rather stripping it of selfishness and self-absorption. Having a faint memory of the perfection of our source, we become fixated on the limitation that is unavoidable in our earthbound dualistic embodiment. Dwelling upon limitation only brings about bitterness and despair, or denial and unhealthy assertion of the ego.

Can you, instead, recognize the strategies of the ego to assert itself; tame the ego by making it humble, sincere, and respectful; and try to find clues about the gifts being offered that are hidden in the mask of self-concept? Instead of destroying it, can you see it as a canvas to work on, a work in progress being remodeled to better reflect your values and your ideal?

Forgetting the self means freeing yourself from the grip of self-absorption, lifting your head from the sand, and recognizing that everyone is caught up in the same kind of struggle with limitation. Behind that drama, spirit is patiently working its way toward self-knowledge and awakening to its unlimited glory.

In the silent life of the tree, spring brings the rising of the sap from the root, and the renewal of the bough. The hope of spring stirs in the bud.

Part II

Bud

INTRODUCTION

The wonderful thing is that the soul already knows to some extent that there is something behind the veil, the veil of perplexity, that there is something to be sought for in the highest spheres of life, that there is some beauty to be seen, that there is Someone to be known who is knowable.

Spiritual progress is the changing of the point of view.
—Hazrat Inayat Khan[1]

So far, I have proposed that your true nature is your soul, and the soul is an expression of universal intelligence, which might be called spirit. It is the nature of spirit to want to know itself; and, over eons, it has been working its way through evolving matter to reach a state of awakening into self-awareness. Each of us has a unique purpose, which is the part we have to play in the awakening of spirit. By following that purpose with trust in the power of spirit to guide us and provide the resources, we are sounding our particular note and coming into harmony with the larger scheme of nature. The guidance of spirit and access to what we need to develop in ourselves is to be found in the inner

1 Inayat Khan, *The Complete Sayings of Hazrat Inayat Khan* (New Lebanon, NY: Omega Publications, 2005), 181; *The Sufi Message,* 10:89

life, which is also called the silent life. A treasure lies in wait for us there.

This part of the book is a travel guide for those who wish to pursue the journey of purpose further. You have everything you need to get started. However, a major expedition requires lots of preparation. We don't want to spend all of our time and energy preparing and never actually set forth. But there is much to do before-hand to make the journey easier and to make success more likely.

The path to realizing your purpose is not an easy one. It requires courage and determination. Consider the example of a great artist. Martha Graham, the legend-ary dancer, gives her testimony about the discipline she chose to follow, to prepare herself to be a channel of excellence for spirit to express itself:

> It takes about ten years to make a mature dancer. The training is twofold. First comes the study and practice of the craft, which is the school where you are working in order to strengthen the muscular structure of the body. The body is shaped, disciplined, honored, and in time, trusted. The movement becomes clean, precise, eloquent, truthful. . . .
>
> Then comes the cultivation of the being from which whatever you have to say comes. It doesn't just come out of nowhere, it comes out of a great curiosity. The main thing, of course, always is the fact that there is only one of you in the world, just one, and if that is not fulfilled then something has been lost....the sweep of life catches up with the mere personality of the performer, and while the individual becomes greater, the personal becomes less personal. And there is grace. I mean the grace resulting from faith. . . .faith in life, in love, in peo-ple, in the act of dancing. All this is necessary to

any performance in life which is magnetic, powerful, rich in meaning.[2]

Martha Graham's experience contains some of the aspects of preparation that will be discussed in this part
of the book. They include self-discipline, preparing the
instrument, surrender to the flow of creativity coming
from within, and trust in the process.

We will begin our preparations by examining our
ways of knowing.

---

2 Martha Graham, "I Am a Dancer," written for the radio program *This I Believe*, published in from *This I Believe*, vol. 2. 1952.

Calling on Intuition

THOUGHT is the way that the mind processes information. The mind can examine, question, analyze or take apart, synthesize or put together, form associations, and come to conclusions. The heart responds to information through feeling. It may react, be triggered, harden or soften, appreciate, be moved, like or dislike, be inspired or disheartened, and it may extend feelings like love, encouragement, tenderness, kindness, compassion, or concern.

Another aspect of feeling might be called sensing. You can sense if a place feels comfortable or stressful. You can feel if an action would be right or wrong. You can sense qualities in a person like honesty, dignity, fortitude, faith, or largeness of heart.

That aspect of yourself that we called *witness* or *spirit* or *intelligence* has another mode of knowing called *intuition*. Intuition can come as unexpected knowledge, as though someone whispered in your ear. You know something, but don't know where that knowledge came from. There are examples of scientists who struggled for years to unravel a mystery and then found the answer symbolically, in a dream or a flash of insight. You might wish ardently for something for a long time, with no sign of progress, and then your wish seems to attract what was needed for success.

Intuition is a flow of insights and creative ideas that comes without mental effort. It does not come from rational or logical analysis. It often comes in a symbolic way, as in a dream or a hunch or an image. It might not reveal its meaning immediately. When you hold it in your mind and remain in a state of suspension, it can bloom as an *aha* moment. Intuition differs from a fantasy, because fantasy is motivated by wish fulfillment or emotional reaction; while with intuition there is a feeling of rightness and appropriateness. It feels like an ingenious answer to the question that evoked it, whether that question was conscious or unconscious. The answer that comes from intuition is often surprising and unexpected. Intuition usually comes more easily to a mind at rest, freed of distractions and the pressures and worries of daily life. Cultivating a period of relaxed silence every day prepares one to seek guidance from intuition.

Intuition can come by becoming familiar with your dreams. By paying attention to dreams, noting them down while they are fresh and pondering their symbolism, you can open up the faculty of intuition. You can also seed a dream by posing a question just before going to sleep, and exploring the symbolic meaning of remembered dreams in relation to the question.

Another way to open up intuition is through creative activity. If you allow creative impulses a life as they arise, you might find unexpected outcomes that reveal insights about your emotional, psychic, or spiritual state. There are many outlets for creativity; for example, spontaneous dancelike movement. Going further, you can pose a question and explore it in some creative medium — dance, music, drama, the plastic arts, ritual, writing, poetry, or other forms.

Another way to access intuition is to commune with nature. You may be able to feel a kinship with an environment, with the rocks and trees, grasses and streams. Nature can speak to you through those impressions that attract your attention. It helps when your senses are keen, and you are aware of the presence of the sensitive life of the organisms all around you. Pir Vilayat Inayat Khan called it *that which transpires behind that which appears*. If you perceive this underlying life, you can be transported by the beauty of what you observe; and nature will communicate with you through signs that otherwise would have escaped your notice. In this way, nature reflects back to you your own aesthetic sensitivity, your values, what you care about. By asking a question of nature, you receive back an echo of the question. The answer to the question was already present in the question. Your conversation with nature helps you to see the answer that was already in you.

Intuition is a gift of the inner life. Make use of that gift and it becomes more available to you.

FINDING A CLUE TO PURPOSE

And how are we to know life's purpose? Can any-
body tell us? No. No one can tell us: for life in its very
nature is self-revealing, and it is our own fault if we
are not open to that revelation which life offers to us.
It is not the fault of life, because the very nature of life
is revealing. Man is the offspring of nature, therefore
his purpose is nature. But the artificiality of life brings
obscurity, which prevents him from arriving at that
knowledge which may be called the revelation of one's
own soul.

And if you ask me how one should proceed, I would
advise you to study every object, whether false or true,
which holds and attracts you, to which you are outward-
ly attracted and also inwardly attracted. And do not
be doubting and suspicious. What Christ taught from
morning till night was faith, but the interpretation of
this word is not made clear. People have said faith in
priest, in church, or in sect. That is not the meaning.
The true meaning of faith is trust in one's self.

— Hazrat Inayat Khan[1]

HOW could we have missed it? Everything is trying to
tell us about our purpose. How is it telling us? By how
it attracts our interest. We may think that our interest
is casual and that it is distracting us from the serious
concerns of life. Maybe we think that what interests

---

1 Inayat Khan, *The Sufi Message*, 10:146.

us is beyond our abilities or beyond our means. We might see it as an impractical pipe dream. We could be afraid to pursue what interests us for fear of failure. We may have tied our self-esteem to being successful, and we're not willing to risk failure with a dream that we can keep alive if we don't test it.

Take heart. If your purpose is what you are meant to do, if there is a greater purpose behind it carrying with it a prodigious power of manifestation, if your love and desire for the object is revealing itself to you, then all that remains is to develop the confidence to own it as your purpose. And how do you develop that confidence? By taking the risks that arise as you step forward, and finding your way to success though you may have to fail again and again.

The interest that might have seemed casual turns out to be central. What could be more important than discovering what you are here to do and going forward with accomplishing it? What is wonderful is that your purpose unfolds in doing what you most love doing.

Humility is needed in posing the question about purpose. We might be moved by the great issues of our time and feel it is our duty to try to bring about some positive change. Following what you love, if it doesn't directly address pressing problems of our time, might seem to some like a cop-out, like sticking your head in the sand. You may truly have a calling to struggle for justice or peace or human rights, but if this is not your calling, your best contribution to serving the good is to sound your true note. Bringing greater harmony and contentment into the psychic atmosphere of the planet serves all other needs. When you sound your note, you are adding something to the symphony of the whole that was missing. As scientists investigate nature, they marvel at the complexity of relationships that are interdependent. The affairs of the world present another complex interconnected network. It is very difficult to decipher what contribution we may be making. We may think that we are a tiny cog in a great machine and what we do or think has negligible influence. It is likely that our angst makes some contribution to the stress of world affairs, and our fulfillment adds to the relief of stress. Though we are indeed a tiny player, we know from Chaos Theory that a tiny influence in an unstable medium can trigger decisive change. By following the path that belongs to you, you are doing your part to bring about a better world for all.

Another question to consider is whether the goal you feel drawn to is worthy of you. Would achieving this goal make you proud? Does it agree with your values? How would it affect others? Does it seem self-serving? Does it reflect psychological needs that should be examined before settling on a goal?

If you are not sure, don't abandon the goal. Your wish is anchored in a deeper wish, one that has a noble purpose. Look more deeply into your wish, seek its roots. Seek the underlying goal that feels honorable.

WISE SELFISHNESS

ONE guideline is clear. The desire that stands out as something you love is the one to follow. However, you may be blessed with many desires. A question you can ask yourself is, *what goal will bring lasting value?* Our society tends to measure value and success by material gains. Have we earned a handsome salary; have we surrounded ourselves with the requisite symbols of material abundance? Our possessions have limited lives. They require maintenance and rob us of our freedom. They may provide comfort and luxury but is that of lasting value?

What is it that adds true value to your life, value that doesn't fade? Whatever builds your confidence, strengthens your faith, and gives lasting satisfaction makes life more meaningful.

There is a give and take in life's experience. For every gain there is a loss and for every loss a gain. Everything has its cost, and nothing, in the end, is lost. Having a success means taking on the responsibility of that success. What have you set in motion? Does it require maintenance? What expectations have you aroused in others? Having raised the bar for yourself, are you now under greater pressure to succeed again? Has your success been at the expense of others? There are many possibilities for a loss resulting from a gain.

On the other hand, a loss may signify the courage to take a risk. If you learn from it, you gain experience and wisdom. You have taken a step toward freeing yourself from the fear of failing. Whatever you own makes its claim on you. When you suffer a loss, you are relieved of the burden of carrying that object.

Some gains are triumphs and carry you to the next step in the unfolding of your purpose. Some losses cause deep bereavement, and work an alchemy on the heart that ultimately awakens a more profound connection to your true desire.

Serving only yourself generally leads, in the end, to disappointment. You are never satisfied with what you can attain for yourself. You always want more.

On the other hand, there is a simple feeling of gratification when you have the opportunity to serve others willingly. It goes beyond the ego's wish to pat itself on the back. It goes beyond a sense of pride in doing good. The Buddhists call it *right aspiration*. You know intuitively when you have done the right thing. The deed in itself gives lasting satisfaction.

Nevertheless, the test of whether your choice of a goal will have lasting value should not be left up to the judging mind. Let it be a feeling deep inside that tells you what is right for you.

SOME COMMON MOTIVATIONS IN LIFE

MANY are the motivations that might guide a person in life. Consider four broad examples. First, there is the person whose desire is to seek wealth and power. Naturally there is a wish in every person for security and comfort. Wealth offers security but also it is the means behind every enterprise. If you want to bring about change for the better in the world, power and wealth can be effective change agents. Many who have gained great wealth through successful enterprise have become agents for good in the world through charitable foundations. The richness of our culture has been promoted by those who have supported schools, hospitals, museums, the arts, and the sciences. Those with a fine sense of beauty have created homes of enduring grace. By collecting or commissioning the works of budding artists, some have continued the tradition of patronage of the arts.

In seeking wealth and power, there is, of course, the danger of greed and domination. After the flush of first success, the ego soon accommodates and begins to take every gain for granted. Then no matter how much you gain, it is never enough. As you gain in power, there is a temptation to feel that you know best. This makes it hard to share power, to listen to and learn from others, to compromise and collaborate. If you are rigid with your power, you invite rebellion and resistance.

Wealth and power can be teachers if we can only learn from their lessons. If you cling to wealth, fearing that you will lose it, you become its servant. Recognizing that your wealth doesn't really belong to you but is given to you in trust, enables you to be generous with it. Then you are in control and you can remember that wealth is a means to an end, not an end in itself.

In a similar way by not letting the fear of losing power control you, you can overcome the competitive impulse to struggle against the power of others. Respecting the power of another, being willing to share power, remembering that your power depends on the respect that others show you, this attitude puts your power at your disposal, not only for accomplishing good, but also for setting an example of harmonious exercise of power.

Taking the chivalric path of duty is a second broad category of motivation. On this path you feel that what is most important in life is to live up to your own ideal. Leading a life of integrity and authenticity is your goal. You would rather lose an advantage than compromise your principles. Life offers many temptations to cut corners, to compromise your standards, to make an exception. On this path you choose to be exacting with yourself, to be uncompromising even in small matters. For the person with this motivation, such a course is the primary consideration. You would rather do what feels right, even if the compromise hardly seems to matter or, on the other hand, if following principle costs dearly. In our sophisticated society where the anti-hero is equated with the common person, we might judge the principled person as unrealistic or too good. There is a nobility in living according to high principles. This path deserves more respect and appreciation. Many feel the longing to rise above the accepted standard and aspire to a nobler way of life. A rebirth of the chivalric ideal is possible in our time. Those who have set an example for humanity by upholding what is just in the face of violent opposition have followed this path.

If you follow this dharmic path, you run the risk of becoming rigid in your principles and judging others whose standard falls beneath your own. There is much sacrifice in sticking to your ideal rather than following your impulse. Resentment toward those who seem to take the easy path could mask itself as arrogance. Despite the great struggle to live nobly, your less than noble feelings could defeat you. By holding high the principle of compassionate understanding, you can find forgiveness for those who are not motivated by duty. Forgiving others doesn't mean indulging them in their neglectfulness. When it seems appropriate, you can help others by calling them on their faults and challenging them to reach higher.

Consider next those whose motivation is to experience all that life has to offer. Only the present moment is real. The past is gone and the future is unknown. If you are on this path, you wish to free yourself from the remorse of the past and the worry of the future. You want to be fully open to seize the promise of what life presents. For example, when you travel, you can plan ahead and stick to the schedule you have made or you can travel without plans, being open to unexpected encounters and circumstances. For the one who prizes living in the moment, freedom is your motto. You embrace every experience, the joy together with the pain. Life becomes a perpetual adventure. I imagine that this motivation requires a certain appetite, an optimistic gusto and a taste for every nuance of experience.

The world offers endless fascination. Much is missed by the timid.

If it is truly the wish of the universal intelligence to know itself through the experience of living in the dualistic, material existence, then the one who follows this path fulfills this wish to the hilt.

The pitfall of this path is that baser tendencies, seeking after pleasures, can lead you into meaningless dissipation. On the path of freedom, of embracing life, you are open to all experiences. You are prepared to try anything. To avoid the pitfall of becoming a slave to pleasure, can you become a connoisseur of experience? By weighing the quality of a pleasure against its cost, you can avoid addictive behavior and digest any experience so that it frees you from its grip. Life can be an artistic pursuit, with each added experience contributing its color and shade to the overall composition.

What about those who become world-weary? By contrast with the seeker after experience, the one who is drawn to this path cares little for the rewards of this world. You long for a different life, a life of purity, solitude, and sacredness. You are homesick for the realm of the soul. It seems as though you have come to this planet from another place, and you feel exiled from your true home. You wish to live a good life of kindness and simplicity while you are here, but want little in return. You live for the next life believing that death is not the end. You wish to resolve affairs in this world as they arise so that you can leave with a clear conscience.

On this path, the risk is that you could become a hermit, isolated and alienated from the larger society. Like those who hold high ideals, you might feel judgmental of others. Or you could become too good for this world, giving freely to others and being taken as naive. You could become the prey of the unscrupulous. Those who feel needy could become attracted to you and latch on to you. With your attention fixed on a more ideal life, you have the opportunity to pass along blessings to all you encounter. Being aware of yourself as a soul, you are more likely to be able to see the souls of others hiding behind their personalities.

If you can remind yourself that the souls of others can manage whatever problems arise, you can free yourself from becoming over-responsible for others, and give blessing and encouragement in place of entanglement.

FULFILLMENT IN RELATIONSHIP

WHEN I consider whether to follow a dream, naturally the question arises: *is it practical?* Can I earn a living and support myself? So you might tend to imagine purpose as a career, as something that results in a valued product.

But what if what calls to you is to be engaged with others, not to produce a particular product but to foster a supportive nurturing relationship? You love to encounter others. You feel enriched, touched, and engaged by getting to know others. Your loneliness is dispelled, your affections are aroused, you feel more alive when you feel close to others.

Perhaps you have a skill in bringing others out. You have patience and a willingness to listen and to discover the hidden gifts of others. You may have an ability to appreciate conflicting points of view. You may have skills as a mediator or as a facilitator who can, by careful listening, draw out the shared vision of a group.

Your purpose could involve some aspect of relationship with others. You might find that through conversation new insights arise and problems are solved. Your confidence in open-ended dialog could be a catalyst for others to open up to this process. You may have an understanding of the dynamics of brainstorming and consensus decision making that helps those processes to be safe and effective.

You may feel a responsibility toward others. For example, you may feel called to serve others in your community, to be outspoken in public meetings, or to take on a responsible role in some aspect of governance. A charity may attract you as a volunteer or as a staff person. Perhaps your purpose involves helping a family member who needs extensive care.

You may also feel that you have a great capacity to love locked up in your heart. Your purpose could be to find a way in this world of prickly egos to unleash that capacity.

Friendship is precious to you. Friendship depends on trust. When you trust another you can achieve a degree of intimacy, feeling truly yourself in the presence of another. You can put aside the social mask, release a level of tension, and feel comfortable just being yourself. Friendship is threatened when trust is broken. It is your responsibility to keep your friend's confidence. When there is a breech of trust, friendship is saved by forgiveness.

Finding a loving partner with whom to share your life is your dream. And raising a family that feels warm and happy is the fulfillment of your loving heart. Friendship is a training ground for a relationship with a partner. When you fall in love, the eyes of your heart are open, and you catch a glimpse of the true nature of the one you love. That is the time to store up the vision of the other's soul. As the relationship matures, the rough edges of the personalities grate against each other, and the vision narrows so that the limitations and shortcomings of the other person come more into focus. When you feel hurt or not seen and react to the other with anger or impatience, that is the time to remind yourself of the true nature of your partner. The vision you saw when your eyes were inspired by fresh love is the unchanging soul of the other person. The personality is a cover over the soul obscuring its light and beauty.

If your purpose lies in the realm of intimate relationship, then your struggle will be to tame your ego so that you can keep your heart soft, open, compassionate, and forgiving. When tension arises, can you melt the heart of your partner by keeping your own heart open? Can you return to intimacy by coming again and again out of hiding, taking the risk to be vulnerable and honest?

Everyone's heart is sensitive, even those who seem cold or tough. The well-defended heart retreats even further when it is challenged. An act of generosity or humility can melt even a heart of ice.

The obstacles on this path are the wounds of a broken or disappointed heart. The heart has a remarkable capacity to heal itself. And it can learn from its wounds. Those wounds can even transform the personality. Working in a detox hospital, I once observed a young man who was struggling with drug addiction returning for the third time from the streets. In his previous stays he had displayed a sharp tongue and a fast-talking cool exterior. On his third admission he was quiet and calm. Yet he radiated a magnetic attraction. Others seemed drawn to him. Through the grapevine I learned that his brother had been shot and killed. His broken heart opened up and warmed the hearts of those around him.

Your purpose is written into your soul; it is your birthright. It has been before you your whole life. The challenge is to trust it and accept it as your own.

Seeking Guidance from the Inner Life

HOW do thoughts arise in the mind? If you observe them forming and dissolving, they seem to arrive spontaneously. Some thoughts seem to be ruminations on the concerns of the day. Others may be triggered by old issues or by sensations that bring about associations with past experiences. Others seem to have no traceable catalysts but appear mysteriously.

Thoughts tend to come to us in language. To express knowledge in language can be a laborious task. A picture can convey information more efficiently. A symbol may contain even more information because it stands for more than a simple picture conveys.

Intuition tends to come as a direct knowing, prior to language. That knowledge is best conveyed in a symbol and, even further, in a symbol or image that is charged with feeling. Knowledge that is experienced with a strong feeling makes a deeper impression. To some degree it can be transformational. If you become inspired or motivated or empowered by an intuition, you feel that you have changed and others notice a change in you.

Access to direct knowing is taught in the Sufi tradition through the practice of concentration, contemplation, meditation, and realization. The novice first learns to concentrate. There is a great benefit in being able to hold the mind steady on a single object. A steady mind allows you to go more deeply into a state of peace and inward absorption. The next stage, when concentration becomes firm, is contemplation. And this stage is followed by meditation. To avoid confusion about these terms, Sufi contemplation is equivalent to Christian meditation or reflection, while Sufi meditation corresponds to Christian contemplation.

Sufi contemplation is a further deepening of the state brought about by concentration. When you can hold the attention steady, then you can focus on an inquiry. Holding a question in the mind, you enter a state of emptiness. By paying attention intently and remaining receptive, you attract the answer, which comes as direct knowledge. It is felt, and may reveal itself as an image or symbol or in some other form that conveys transformative information.

By turning within, entering a peaceful silence, making yourself empty and receptive, holding a question, and staying alert for a response, you can receive guidance or intuitive knowledge. It is not what the mind would have offered. It is not a logical response to the question. It comes as a leap beyond the mind. It comes as a gift. It comes from the realm of love and light, which you can experience when you become at home in the silence.

How you approach the silence makes a difference. Set aside a time when you won't be bothered by any distractions. If you can, choose a place that is peaceful, comfortable, and makes a pleasant or uplifting impression. You could use flowers or artwork to create an atmosphere. Though your eyes are closed, you will take in the feeling of the space around you just before you close your eyes.

Treat the inner life as your personal temple, a sacred place. When you close your eyes, you could imagine a beautiful place, an ideal landscape, a site that has a sacred feeling. Then you could try imagining light and love on each breath, to ward off disturbing thoughts.

If you find your mind wandering into a dream state, starting to digest old impressions or events, or planning for the future, just notice the mental activity, let it be; but turn your attention back to breathing peacefully and filling the inner space with light and love. Enjoy the vacation from mental activity, no matter how brief.

When you are ready, formulate a question as clearly as you can. It can be a broad question such as: *help me find a clue to my purpose in life*, or a very specific question such as: *what is the next step I need to take in my life to move toward my life's goal?* The more specific the question, the more specific the guidance is likely to be.

Once you have decided on the question, simply hold it in mind and relax. Let go of the impatience to find an answer. Clear your mind of any preconceptions about the answer. Let yourself go blank, without any notion of an answer, remaining in suspension. If any anxieties arise in this state, release them through the breath and relax. Tell yourself that you trust the answer will come, and you are opening yourself to receive it. If you notice your mind trying to present rational answers, dismiss them and remain open.

On the other hand, if you notice a dreamlike impression coming, an image, a symbol, a sound, an impression, pay attention even if the impression seems to have nothing to do with the question. As you pay attention, follow the impression without judging it to see how it develops. Don't try to interpret it but just let it play out. Before trying to analyze it, notice the feeling state it brings about. If you feel touched, moved, elated, amused, delighted, or some other strong feeling, this is a sign that there is an answer to your question hidden in what you observed and felt.

Intuition responds like a person to being courted. Don't forget to thank that faculty for whatever it produced. If you truly appreciate your intuition, it will be more likely to respond strongly next time.

Preparations

WHAT are the basic resources needed to accomplish what our inner voice is urging us to do? We have been given an exquisite instrument: a body and a mind. Imagine how many eons it has taken to evolve an organism that is so sensitive and so complex. We take the body and mind for granted. Our modern lifestyle tends to squander those gifts. Yet maintenance and upkeep for this extraordinary mechanism doesn't require much effort. The first thing to examine is how well you are taking care of your body. A reasonable diet and regular exercise should be sufficient unless your path requires athletic skills.

What about the mind? There is so much stimulation in our culture that our minds tend to be busy throughout the day and even well into the night. We may not be aware of the strain on the nervous system that constant agitation brings. Stress seems to be a universal ailment. There are many specific methods for stress reduction. A more basic approach would be to educate ourselves and our children about healthier lifestyle habits. We are out of balance. The health of both body and mind rely on balance in activity and rest. We may think that less serious activity, such as entertainment or recreational sport, counts as rest from the activity we would call work. Although relaxation and enjoyment are steps in the right direction, the mind and nervous system need periodic time-outs. The mind needs peace and quiet. After a peaceful sleep, the mind is refreshed; your spirit is renewed. But sleep will be disturbed when the day goes by without a break. It takes time for the nerves to calm down after stimulation. And the mind automatically processes daily impressions as soon as it gets a chance. There is no place in our daily life for doing nothing.

We are so used to feeding our minds with sensations, worries, dramas, facts and opinions, and puzzles, that when we take time to actually rest the mind, the first thing that happens is that we feel bored. Then, if that isn't enough, unresolved feelings that we have avoided through a steady diet of distractions may come bobbing to the surface. How can we rest the mind and nerves if agitation seems to be our default state? How can we find peace?

A way to deal with boredom is to find pleasure in silence and solitude. I have suggested a practice of the imagination to fill the inner space with light or love. At first this altered state may only last for seconds. With practice the inner experience becomes real; it draws you in, and you can simply enjoy it without any effort to sustain it.

How about painful or uncomfortable material that rises up in the silence? The best way to deal with undesired impressions is to face them and see what can be done with them.

I have already talked about conscience, a faculty that records thoughts, feelings, and actions that don't match up with our innate sense of values. When we experience something that goes against our sense of right and wrong, if we don't deal with it, it becomes a weight in the conscience, a burden we carry through life. It makes everything harder. By examining the conscience and facing up to what it contains, there is a possibility of lightening our load. Every step in relieving the conscience brings us closer to a state of peace.

If we can view painful memories, negative feelings about ourselves, antagonisms towards others, and those feelings that weigh down our conscience, through the eyes of the Witness, if we can see ourselves objectively, as we would view another person, then there is a chance for resolving those disturbing and weakening impressions. We can take the actions needed to make amends where we have made mistakes. We can learn from our faults and begin to correct them. We can resolve to break demoralizing habits. We can do the reparative work on our attitude and self-esteem that will free us to focus constructive attention on our purpose.

Preparing to make a wholehearted effort to fulfill one's purpose is like training as an athlete. It requires discipline and optimism. Every step taken in that direction gives you a feeling of growing strength and happiness.

Narrowness and Vastness

SYMBOLICALLY, the Sufis picture the nature of the human as a string, one end of which is fixed in ordinary life and the other end of which is infinite. The fixed end is our usual notion of our self as limited and constrained, isolated and tiny in the larger scheme of things, one among billions. We barely know the other end, unlimited, free, vast, and mysterious. Its lack of boundaries, the impossibility of defining it, the vagueness of our experience of it, means that it is scary for some. Can we believe that it is real?

There is an ancient story about the first human: Adam. As a soul, he refused to enter the body of clay, which to him seemed like a tiny prison. The Creator commanded the angels to sing. Transported by the music and moved to dance, the soul of Adam entered the body and became the first human being.

This story describes our condition. We have a memory and an ongoing subliminal awareness of being a soul, of feeling utterly free and vast, of exulting in unlimited light and love. But our reality is living in the narrowness of the prison, not only of a body vulnerable to illness, injury, and decline, but also the narrowness of our little self.

The promise of finding purpose and meaning in life is a reminder that what appears to be our impoverished reality is not all that it seems. Our exploration of silence and the inner life, begins to open the door to reconnecting with the seminal state of soul.

We have been speaking of a universal intelligence that animates all life and takes us as its instrument. Now let us add a further subtlety to that picture. Like the soul of Adam, our true self is a vast soul, which has entered the tininess of our presumed self, in order to experience life and unfold and know something of its hidden nature.

Is soul different from spirit, from the universal intelligence? Yes and no. The difference is like comparing a ray of sunlight with the sun. Although the ray is not the light of the whole sun, there is no boundary between the ray and the rest of the light. Where does the ray leave off from the rest of the light of the sun? The ray is seamlessly a part of the whole light. One might even say that the light of the whole sun comes through the ray.

Entering the silence, observing your life as the Witness, and calling on intuition to guide you, are ways to get to know and work with your purpose. Another way has been called by the Sufis, *tuning to the infinite*.

How can you tune to the experience of the infinite? One way is to use your imagination to shuttle back and forth between two perspectives. Sit quietly with your back upright and watch the breath going in and out. Relax as much as possible and don't pay attention to stray thoughts. When you breathe in, think of drawing your awareness down to a point in the center of your body. We speak of centering our self when we feel scattered, our attention going in many directions at once. When you draw your attention down to a point, notice the feeling of being centered or one-pointed.

When you breathe out, imagine scattering your attention out into interstellar space. Imagine the vastness of the space between stars. Imagine that you have no center any more, but you are spread out in space and your self is vast like the space itself. Breathing in, imagine drawing that feeling of vastness and freedom back down into a point at the center of the body.

You continue this shuttling back and forth between centeredness and vastness for as long as you feel comfortable doing it. If you do this exercise daily for a while, your memory of the vast dimension of yourself may begin to return.

Need for Sacredness

MODERN life, with all its conveniences, advanced medicine, abundance of foods, networks of communication, knowledge at our fingertips, ease of travel, richness of arts and culture, and scientific discoveries, still lacks something very basic: a need for sacredness. We might find it in a religious service, a moment of awe in nature, a major life transition, or an opening of the heart when it is touched. Though it is always there, available to us, the fast rhythm of modern life tends to intoxicate us, and we miss it. We gravitate toward excitement and stimulation to relieve a feeling of flatness and routine. Some cultures have incorporated religious ritual, prayers, and sacred art into daily life. For those societies, reminders of sacred presence are never far from daily activities.

If you are in a natural environment and take a moment to observe closely the beauty of nature, you may feel as though you are waking up after a long period of sleepwalking. When you become aware of a feeling of awe or wonder, your feeling of being awake and alive is enhanced.

What would it take to wake up, and all the time be aware of the wonder and mystery of being alive? If you become aware that your life has a purpose, that you have been given the gifts needed to achieve that purpose, and that the intelligence that animates the whole creation is working through you to bring about something beautiful, then how can you go back to sleep again?

Your life and all life reveals that it is full of meaning. Every purpose is a sacred trust. It needs protection and attention. Like a seed, it will grow to fruition by itself if it gets sun, good soil, and watering. The sun is your loving attention. Good soil is the result of careful preparation of you as an instrument to perform the task. Watering is the flow of guidance and inspiration that comes from faith in your purpose, faith in the power behind it, and openness to receive what is given.

The soul, the essence of *who I am*, is starving for a regular diet of sacredness. Without it, your deepest inner life feels arid, dried up, dead. For some, religion provides the soul's nourishment. For others, it might come from loving ties to family and friends. Some may find it in living close to nature. For some, adventure and discovery might be a steady source of wonder and awe. There are many ways to find sacredness in life. Awakening to your purpose will probably reaffirm those sources of sacred experience that you have naturally discovered.

We have an inherent sacredness waiting to be discovered. When we wake up to that feeling of grace, we become aware of sacredness everywhere, in our loved ones, in everyone we meet, and in every aspect of nature.

KNOWING YOUR VALUES

WE live in an age of moral relativism. We know that different cultures have different moral codes. We are sophisticated enough to know that our code, though it feels right for us, is not to be imposed on another culture. We have come to respect a diversity of moralities.

When we look at morals more closely, we can see that there is also a situational relativism. To lie to save a life is very different than to lie to protect one's interests or to promote oneself.

Within a culture, though there may be a generally accepted sense of morality, there is a lot of latitude for individual variations.

Where do our values come from? We learn values from family, parents and grandparents, from religious and social influences, from school, from associates, from figures we admire. We might think that our values are all externally imposed. If those values have been impressed on us in a harsh or punitive way, we might feel inclined to rebel.

In reality, the only meaningful values in our lives are the ones we own. We have an inherent sense of values. We know them intuitively because they feel right. When we admire what we see in others, we are discovering our own inherent values. By becoming aware of those values and owning them, we no longer need to rebel.

Once we free ourselves of imposed values, we don't have to feel compelled to impose our values on others.

We function in this world of duality as limited beings. Our true nature can only be understood from the perspective of unity. From that point of view, we are instruments for perfect intelligence or spirit seeking to know itself. However, functioning in the world of duality we make mistakes, we fall short of our values. This is natural.

Being self-critical or remorseful about our faults is counterproductive. Our mistakes are opportunities for growth if we can own up to them. Our daily challenge is to try to better live up to our values. In doing so, we strive for greater perfection, according to the admonition of Jesus: "Be ye therefore perfect, even as your Father which is in heaven."[1]

The challenge of living up to our values comes when they do not seem to serve our self-interest. If we always strive to live up to our highest values, we may have to sacrifice our own interest. Our security may seem to be at stake. It is our sense of inner security that is being tested. If we are going to take the noble path, we will need faith that doing the right thing, the thing that feels right, will be in our best interest.

That strength comes when the heart is open and you are willing to take the risk of being betrayed or deceived. Can you see the long-term benefit of being true to what you hold dear, over the short-term benefit of playing the game of getting ahead? Can you value the riches of an unburdened conscience and the peacefulness of a sturdy self-esteem over the unstable security that you gain by playing it safe?

What do I care most about in life? Where do I want to put my efforts, what do I want to contribute? How

---

1 Matthew 5:48.

do I want to be? I may take my personality as just the way I am. For the Sufis, developing the personality according to one's values is an art. I can use my aesthetic sense to polish my manners, to foster an attitude toward myself and others that earmarks beauty. The Sufis have identified respect as a key to reshaping the personality. Respect for yourself and respect for others springs from awakening to the sacredness that gives all of us life. If we can look beyond the surface of limitation into the depth of perfection, we can perceive the underlying beauty in ourselves and in everyone we encounter. Inspired by that beauty, our personality can become graceful, harmonious, and generous. A beautiful personality will attract blessing and success.

Opening your heart, trusting in the larger forces at work, and living up to your values, are important preparations to make for the journey of fulfilling your purpose.

Unlearning

PREPARING for a journey, it is customary to learn all we can about where we are going, the geography, history, culture, interesting sites, language, customs, and cuisine. Without that preparation we might feel at a loss, wandering aimlessly. We are accustomed to relying on our minds and seeking information externally to guide our minds. When it comes to purpose, the mind is a limiting factor. We have to engage our whole self, and this requires inspiration.

Where does inspiration come from? It comes from within. Because we generally believe that good decisions depend on thinking, our tendency is to seek more knowledge. If only we had sufficient knowledge, we would know what we are supposed to do or be. More often than not, that kind of knowledge gets in the way. To discover inspiration, the first step is to open up to all possibilities. That means clearing away all preconceptions. All that you have learned about life, about how the world works, about yourself—now the challenge is to unlearn it all. The subtle voices in your mind that say, *no, not possible,* have to be stilled. The framework that has made sense of life up to now—are you ready to abandon it for the possibility of greater insight?

The Sufis have described the process of inspiration as the pouring of a deeper knowledge into an empty vessel. If the vessel is filled with conventional knowledge, with presumptions, assumptions, doctrines, and dogmas, there is no room for knowledge that comes spontaneously from within.

How do you go about unlearning all that you have acquired in life? One way is to practice adopting the point of view of another. This can be very useful in resolving conflicts. If you find yourself on one side of a conflict, you may notice that you tend to belittle your opponents. Can you put yourself in their shoes and try to see why they think the way they do? Can you defend the other point of view and be critical of your own view? Doing so begins to loosen your attachment to your preconceptions. There may be a bit of a wrenching feeling in relaxing strongly held opinions. But it is this feeling of relaxing your grip on everything you thought was true that points the way toward unlearning.

When we try to get into the mind of someone we disagree with, we may discover the emotional underpinning of our strongly held belief. We may cling to some ideas because they give us a feeling of security. Without the structure of certain beliefs, we might feel at the mercy of a chaotic world where anything is possible. Beliefs that have an emotional grip on us may result in rigidity. We may not be willing to listen to other points of view.

Unlearning means overcoming rigidity and adopting openness and receptivity. Any ideas, no matter how contrary to what we assume, we can examine calmly and consider their merits. This state of calm patience and willingness to see the positive side of something new prepares one to receive an inspiration.

When an inspiration comes, we may block it because we think it is impractical or we feel we are too limited to carry it out. Unlearning also means putting aside our negative judgments about ourselves, and trusting that the gift of inspiration has been given to us because it is ours to fulfill. Perhaps this is the most difficult aspect of unlearning. Can we see that the social construct we think is our self is a mirage? Can we trust that the Hidden Treasure is seeking our help to discover itself by inspiring us to act or to be?

SELF-DISCIPLINE

IF you are fortunate enough to live in a prosperous culture, the temptations for instant gratification are legion. The comforts of modern life shield us from the everyday struggles of a simple life close to nature. So is it any wonder that we are not prepared to take ourselves in hand, control our impulses, endure hardship, or overcome obstacles? We are generally protected as children and, when it comes to everyday needs, we are used to having what we want or think we want.

To embark on a serious quest to achieve something meaningful, developing mastery over oneself is crucial. Setting out with a glorious vision of what you would like to accomplish, you will soon encounter obstacles. Without the determination, resourcefulness, and confidence that the practice of mastery provides, you are likely all to succumb too soon.

How can you develop mastery? Not by dwelling on failures. On the contrary, you have to be ready to fail again and again. Of course every failure is an opportunity to learn something. If you can free yourself from identifying with a failure, if you can see it with detachment, then it becomes a stimulus to growth.

You can train yourself in mastery by doing things that oppose your habits or conventions. For example, you could eat when not hungry and not eat when hungry.

You could rest when wanting to be active and be active when you want to rest. If there is something you resist doing, you could do it without hesitation. You just decide to do it and go ahead, ignoring the mind's objections. Or you could use restraint to stop yourself from doing something you would like to do.

When there is something to do and you don't feel like doing it, your mind tells you it can wait. Decide then to do it anyway. See what feelings come up, resistance, fear, annoyance, tiredness. Let the feelings be there but don't let them stop you. When you have completed the task, these feelings will likely go away. They may be replaced by feelings of satisfaction, peace, and contentment.

Longstanding habits are difficult to dislodge. You may not want to attempt to change a habit until you have gained some strength and confidence with simpler challenges. When you do try to master a habit you want to get rid of, don't be discouraged by repeated failures. You may have invested many years in establishing a habit. It will take patience and persistence to uproot it.

What can happen is that because the feeling of overcoming is so exhilarating, you start to look for more opportunities to challenge yourself. You begin to feel confidence in your power of self-control. This can translate into confidence in facing obstacles and persistence in overcoming them even through many failures.

When we are not in control of our impulses, we feel like a slave. When we develop self- control, we become the master of life.

The greatest obstacle you will meet on the path to accomplishing your purpose is your limited sense of yourself. Seeking comfort and security, that limited self, sometimes called the ego, resists sacrifice, whole-hearted effort, risk-taking, and lacks faith in your calling. As long as you identify with the resisting ego, you remain a servant to its needs. By discovering the experience of mastery over yourself, you make the ego your servant. Then the way opens to overcoming the most difficult obstacles on your path. Much work remains to be done, but you have in your hand the leverage you need to prevail.

WILL POWER

SELF-CONTROL is the assertion of conscious steering of the self around the shoals of immediate gratification. When you have a specific goal and actively pursue it, you are exercising will power.

In the adventure of finding and fulfilling your purpose, the first step is recognizing your desire. That longing is an ever-present resonance in the background. When it is brought to the surface, it emerges from a generalized feeling and becomes more specific as a wish. Then you know what you want. At first the wish is delicate like the tender shoot of a plant springing from a seed. It needs protection from any influence that might bring discouragement or doubt. For this reason, it is best to keep silent about your discovery, even though there is a great temptation to share your excitement. Sharing can happen when the shoot becomes established as a sturdy plant.

In order for the plant to grow, wish must generate will, the determination to make it happen regardless of the difficulties you might encounter. In the days of chivalry, when one committed one's word, one was honor bound to fulfill one's commitment, no matter what the consequences. To catalyze the transition from wish to will, it is helpful to make a pledge to yourself. If you can make that pledge into a simple statement and say it out loud, you will impress your mind and heart with the commitment you are making. Repeating the pledge to yourself periodically helps to reinforce the will.

It is also important to remind yourself frequently that your desire is a personalized version of a greater desire: the desire of universal intelligence to know itself. Your wish is an expression of the wish of spirit, and your will and commitment are backed by the will of the underlying intelligence behind the whole universe. As Jesus said, "Thy will be done on earth as it is in heaven."[1] It is strengthening to realize that your pledge and your will is helping to bring to fruition a larger will and, vice versa, that a larger will is backing up your will and helping you to succeed with your desire.

Some who have had a strict upbringing or were heavily criticized as children might find it painful at first to try to live up to a pledge. The best remedy is to remember that the growth required to fulfill your goal comes from a willingness to fail again and again, each time learning the lesson.

Will power is developed by practicing mastery. By not giving in to your whim or impulse, you are exercising a muscle. Over time that muscle will grow strong. It will become easier to control your impulses, and also to overcome resistance with determined action.

Is it not possible that will power could become too strong or too rigid? By plunging ahead no matter what the consequences, you could cause destruction for others and for yourself. The unbowed spirit does not accept defeat, but this attitude can also become distorted. If you cannot bend with adversity, rigid pride could cause you to break. Strengthening will power is an art,

---

1 Matthew 6:10.

and the artist's sensitivity to beauty will ensure a harmonious outcome.

There is a greater and a lesser will. The will you bring to bear through your commitment and determination is the lesser will. When it is aligned with the greater will, things go smoothly, doors open. The greater will always prevails in the end, but there is room for your personal will to get off track. That's when it can become destructive.

How do you know if your will is in harmony with the will of the spirit or universal intelligence? Can you sit in stillness, become peaceful, and sense deeply inside whether what you are doing feels right? Be wary of mental justifications. If your conscience is at ease, and you are fully comfortable with where your will is taking you, then it is likely that your will agrees with the larger will.

Make Peace in Your Life

Isn't it enough to answer the demands of life, to be self-supporting, to meet the responsibilities for family and friends, and to be a contributing citizen to your community and country? Yes, if that life gives you satisfaction, then there is no reason to seek something more. Then you have found your purpose.

But if you have a nagging feeling that there is more to life, if you wonder whether at the end of life you will feel that you missed an opportunity, then you may be ready to face the challenges of finding and living a purpose that has not yet become clear.

In the early stages of this journey, you may become intoxicated with inspiration. You may envision grand success and daydream about it. As soon as you take the first steps to make the dream a reality, you are confronted by your own limitations. Can I do this? Do I have the courage, strength, and persistence to keep going when I falter? Familiar inner struggles are amplified, unresolved issues will come up. You will need to summon all of your fortitude and determination.

How much time and energy do you spend each day reacting to those who irritate you or push your buttons? Even if you don't react outwardly, there is the inner reaction, the preoccupation with an upsetting interaction that may go on long afterwards. We can waste our inner resources on blaming and judging others or on criticizing ourselves. There is a way to reduce the stress in your outer life. Jesus tells us to turn the other cheek and to love our enemies. How can we do that when our instant reaction is to fight back outwardly or inwardly, or to collapse inside?

The Buddhists have given us a powerful tool for dealing with reactions. It sounds very simple but it is surprisingly effective. If you can simply become aware of your reaction when it is happening, you begin to disarm it. There is no judgment in this awareness, no thought that I shouldn't be reacting. By observing yourself, you are taking a step toward becoming objective, a step toward freeing yourself from the emotional grip of the reaction. This is similar to the practice of the Witness.

When you begin to loosen your identification with the reaction, you gain insight into it. You begin to see why you are reacting. Once you see the cause, the possibility of not having to react opens up. You have a choice to be proactive instead of reactive. Instead of instinctively protecting your wounds, you can choose to respond to the hurt of the person who is triggering you. You can choose to take the blow and not feed the fire by escalating.

Wherever there is tension and conflict in the outer life, you can do your best to make peace. If you feel provoked, you can decide not to rise to the bait. Let the other person get the last word or win an argument or behave badly. By not engaging you save yourself from escalation and aggravation. It may feel hard not to answer back, but it doesn't really matter if the other person seems to win. It's a hollow victory. Your dignity doesn't depend on appearances. Remember that nothing can touch your inner dignity. If you can forgive those who irritate you and forgive yourself for annoying others, you will significantly reduce the emotional burden of the day; and you will be left with energy to confront the inner issues of confidence and patience.

When relationships trigger insecurities, we get drained. Learning to stay calm and witness those insecurities with a bit of humor can make our outer life significantly easier. You can reserve your energy to engage in mastering the impulses of the ego.

Fear and Faith

WHEN you turn your attention to what is most meaningful to you, the first response is probably excitement and enthusiasm. Your imagination provides you with a beautiful vision of what success could look like. You dream of an ideal fulfillment. You can already taste the satisfaction of bountiful success. Holding this vision can help you persist through difficulties.

As soon as you begin to take steps towards your goal, however, the obstacle that immediately arises is creeping self-doubt. From that shadow of doubt all sorts of fears can emerge. Can I do this? Is it too hard? Do I deserve it? Will I embarrass myself? Am I being selfish? Is life just too restrictive? Am I a victim of fate? The feeling tends to settle in the abdomen as tightness, as pressure, as queasiness, as restlessness. Emotionally, one feels anxious, vulnerable, and irritable. The mind amplifies the feeling with scenarios of fear or dread.

If fear goes unchecked, progress is blocked. Excitement and momentum come to a halt. You close down. With fear that only arises occasionally, you can continue to function. When fear becomes a preoccupation it leads into depression, a state in which it is very difficult to function. It is a kind of death in life. One is cut off from motivation. All forward progress has stopped. One is stuck and can't see a way out.

Doubt is a shadow that leads toward darkness. Confidence moves in the direction of light. A friend once told me of an experience he had on an LSD trip. He was going into a dark nightmarish state. Someone came by and put a finger in front of his face, which had been cast down. The passerby slowly lifted his finger, and my friend followed it, lifting his face upward. The clouds parted and he found himself in a landscape of light.

Helen Keller, living in a sensual world of darkness and silence, had to make the choice between regarding the world as darkness or light. In "Dreams That Come True," she gives her point of view.

> There is something divine in the art which some human beings possess to shape life for themselves, no matter what the outward circumstances may be. That is the power of the Celestial Artist, the Will, to find life worth living, despite the handicap imposed. I have for many years endeavored to make this vital truth clear; and still people marvel when I tell them that I am happy. They imagine that my limitations weigh heavily upon my spirit, and chain me to the rock of my despair. Yet, it seems to me, happiness has very little to do with the senses. If we make up our minds that this is a drab and purposeless universe, it will be that and nothing else. On the other hand, if we believe that the earth is ours, and that the sun and moon hang in the sky for our delight, there will be joy upon the hills and gladness in the fields, because the Artist in our souls glorifies creation. Surely, it gives dignity to life to believe that we are born into this world for noble ends, and that we have a higher destiny than can

be accomplished within the narrow limits of this physical life.[1]

Where does confidence come from? Confidence comes from success, from discovering that you have abilities that you previously didn't know about. So long as we are able to do what others around us can do, we develop a healthy sense of confidence. Then we begin to identify with those skills that set us apart: I'm smart or I'm pretty or graceful or athletic. And then we may also identify with negative attributes: I'm clumsy, I'm slow, I'm unattractive. Do we own the skills that give us confidence? Because they came easily to us doesn't mean that we can take credit for them. And those attributes we feel bad about, is it our fault if we fall short compared to another? We are the way we came into the world. Each person has received certain gifts and certain handicaps. Both the gifts and the handicaps are designed to serve your purpose. How they serve is a puzzle for us to solve through intuition, through a deeper understanding.

When we identify with positive or negative attributes, we presume to own them. We are blind to the intelligence that has shaped us this way, that has given us gifts and challenged us to bring out our latent strengths. We can see this more clearly if we step back from preoccupation with whether we are OK or not. When we can see ourselves objectively from the perspective of the Witness, we may discover how we are truly suited to the purpose that slowly reveals itself to us.

Doubt comes from an experience of failure, real or imagined. Whether we regard the experience as a failure or not may depend on the evaluation of others. If we

1 Helen Keller, "Dreams That Come True" *Personality* (December, 1927).

have taken in negative impressions from the reactions of others, then we are conditioned to doubt ourselves. But failure needn't be a cause for doubt.

> *I regard every failure as a steppingstone to a success.*
> — Hazrat Inayat Khan[2]

Success and failure can work in two ways. They both affect the gut. Success gives a feeling of freedom and expansion in the gut. We feel poised and balanced at the center of the body, and we gather strength of will that we also feel in that place. Success can be taken personally, in which case we may feel proud and, perhaps, inflated, making us vulnerable to a fall or deflation. Or success can be impersonal and increase our faith in the unseen help we received, which made the success possible.

Failure hits us in the gut and produces the feelings of contraction and anxiety described earlier. When it feels personal, failure casts us into the darkness of self-doubt, into negative self-image. But when we take failure impersonally, we discover that this is how we learn. We can't expect to be successful every time we try something. We learn by trial and error. Next time we do it differently and, if we don't give up, we keep trying until we find the way that succeeds.

If you have been conditioned to see things negatively or to hold a negative self-image, can you shift your attention from the darkness to the light? If you are looking down, absorbed in how you are doing, in rating yourself, then you can train yourself to look upwards towards the light. That means seeing the larger picture. Success is a gift for which you can be thankful. Failure is a lesson which, if you learn from it, will guide you to success, to self-confidence, to faith.

---

2 Inayat Khan, *The Sufi Message* 5: 252.

You can't choose to have faith or doubt. This is what you experience. Your attitude toward your experience can gradually change the balance toward more faith and less doubt.

An actor experiences fear just before going onstage as the nervous condition called *butterflies in the stomach*. In those tense moments of waiting, of having to remain immobile, self-doubt seizes the opportunity to haunt the mind. But that period of waiting is also like the archer drawing back the bow. And when the actor goes onstage, the arrow is released. Now there is no time for worry or dread; every moment becomes vivid. The potential energy built up by fear now becomes a flood of kinetic energy. Time seems to slow down. There is time to correct for mistakes. The moment is plastic.

Perhaps you have had the experience of jumping from rock to rock to cross a stream. Your mind tries to plot a course, but once you are in the air, your body's intelligence takes over. Again time seems to expand so that you have a moment in mid-air to make last minute corrections.

We would like to figure out ahead of time a clear path to success. But fear arises when we doubt our ability to tread that path without stumbling. Faith seems to come when we take the risk to step forward, bypassing the mind and surrendering to a kinetic responsiveness that operates faster than the mind. The mind finds security in holding rigidly to a plan. Our improvisational capability is flexible. It adapts to conditions as they arise. It surprises us with responses we would never have imagined.

Fear is the absence of motion. Sometimes all that is needed to release it, is movement in some direction. It doesn't seem to matter what direction one takes. Motion begets motion. The impulse that fear has locked up wishes for freedom. Faith, once unleashed, has a vitality and irrepressibility that comes as a gift and a surprise.

We don't realize what we are sitting on. Fear is a contraction that makes us feel diminished. All along, coming from the unseen, there is a boundless source of creativity targeting us as its hope for expression.

We come into this life in a state of openness. A child readily believes when it is taught something. Children live in a natural state of faith. A child has trust in its caregivers, trust in nature, trust in itself. As an adult, we regard that childlike state of faith as naive. We have learned through hard experience that life and others are not so easily to be trusted. And further, we have lost trust in ourselves. The disappointing experiences have become like so many clouds obscuring the sunny sky of our childhood faith. Yet, like the sun behind the clouds, that innate faith is still there. If we can penetrate the clouds, we will find that our original faith is still intact.

> *Befool not, O night, the morn will break;*
> *Beware, O darkness, the sun will shine;*
> *Be not vain, O mist, it will once more be clear;*
> *My sorrow, forget not, once again joy will arise.*
> — Hazrat Inayat Khan[3]

How does one penetrate the clouds? Clouds can be burned away by the heat of the sun. They can be blown away by rising winds. And they can dissipate by dropping their load of rain, leaving behind a freshness in the earth. The burning action of the sun is the effect of the passionate gaze of an opened and sympathetic heart. The blowing of the wind is the marshaling of will power to act rightly, according to one's highest

3 Inayat Khan, *The Complete Sayings of Hazrat Inayat Khan*, 173.

values. And the release of the rain is the full expression of one's grief over life's pain and suffering, which is followed by a flowing of love from an awakened heart.

Faced with one's persistent shortcomings, wisdom seeks a balance between two aspects of faith. On the one hand, you need freedom from the debilitating effect of harsh self-criticism. This can happen through radical acceptance. Can you look calmly and objectively at your faults, refraining from judgments or rationalizations? You accept without excuse your shortcomings, owning them, becoming transparent and feeling seen by the eye of unconditional love. You trust that you are seen sympathetically and loved for who you are. You have trust in the unseen spirit that is the source of all individual beings.

On the other hand, you accept full responsibility for those faults, vowing to replace them to the best of your ability by the way you wish to behave. You have faith in yourself to struggle with habits and impulses, to control yourself and to reach for an ideal that is meaningful and authentic for you.

These two aspects of faith give you support and also build confidence and self-respect.

If an artist was able to paint with only light, we would not be able to make out the picture. We can only appreciate the light when it is framed by shades and shadows. Music that uplifts us often combines dark tones of sadness or despair with a breakthrough of sunlight or renewal. To appreciate joy we have to experience pain, to know hope we must have passed through grief. Without fear, we would have no word for faith. It would be our natural state, but we would have only the most superficial awareness of it.

Fear has a role to play in life. In situations where it is warranted, it alerts us to imminent harm. When the warning of harm is overblown or imaginary, when what we are protecting doesn't really need protection, then the role of fear is to bring out our latent courage. Fear is a practice dragon for fledgling knights. Defeat this dragon and be invested with the dignity of knighthood.

Knighthood on the one hand is a sign of bravery. On the other hand, we picture the knight kneeling in humility, blessed by the rays of light coming through the stained glass windows of a chapel.

Defeating the dragon of fear brings you pride and confidence in your strength. At the same time, if you remember that your strength is a gift from an unseen source beyond your control, you bow your head in humility. Fear is replaced by faith in yourself and faith in hidden help.

An artist, absorbed in his or her work, might emerge at some point and wonder, did I create this? Where did it come from? The creative process seems to flow from somewhere beyond the mind. Anyone fully absorbed in an activity might have this experience. It is as though there is a creative jinn who takes over in moments of abstraction and guides the hand of the artist or athlete or any kind of actor on life's stage.

Do we become possessed by spirits when we create? You might experience it this way. There is another way to look at it. The essential *I*, the pure intelligence that accounts for the feeling that I exist, is continually flowing into me. There is a steady stream of thoughts, feelings, and impulses that are clearly perceptible and tangible in our experience. Usually we go through life identifying this flow as our individual idiosyncrasy. We are propelled by it but don't really know what to make of it. If we became more aware of that flow as intentional rather than random, as proceeding from our essential life source, from a perfect intelligence seeking to know itself through our experience, what would this mean for our faith?

First of all we would discover the reality of a meaningful flow of purpose and desire. We would gain faith in the meaningfulness of our life and in the source of guidance and creative imagination within us.

And we would realize that as an artist of life, we have a role to play in shaping that flow of creativity to produce something beautiful, according to our aesthetic sense. Our self-confidence, our faith in our self, arises from the part we can play as the partner and the instrument of a downpouring of inspiration.

Inspiration

FACE-to-face with the task you have chosen to pursue, you might find yourself at a loss about how to proceed. Where can you find the inspiration for the next step? Whatever step you imagine taking seems pedestrian, uninspired. To engage in something that gives meaning to your life brings out your highest standards. It cannot be business as usual, because it is something you care greatly about. How do you find inspiration to go forward with enthusiasm? How do you get beyond feeling stuck?

Here are some steps that have helped me. First, can you open your heart to love your task? Fear, insecurity, and self-judgment cause a contraction in the heart. If you begin to feel your commitment as a burden, your task as a confining duty, then you are losing the joy and privilege of actually doing what has been given to you to do. Remind yourself daily that this task is a gift and that you are the person to carry it out. Rise above discouraging feelings and fear. Rising above feelings doesn't mean denying them. Recognize those feelings, accept them, and witness them but lift your spirits. Be aware of the vastness of the world and of the stars and galaxies. In the vast theater of the glorious creation, how important are your worries and fears? They are here today and gone tomorrow. Take heart. Your love for the task is more important and more powerful than any sense of limitation you feel.

Second, trust in the desire behind your desire. The all-pervading intelligent spirit is the source of your desire. Endless inspiration is waiting for you to open to its call. It needs a clear channel, freed of the congestion of doubt and fear. Clarity and openness come with calmness and relaxation. Replace striving and pushing yourself with trusting and patience.

Third, if you feel stuck, if you reject every impulse as insufficient, then you can override your scruples to generate some motion. Go ahead with any impulse, it doesn't matter what. As discussed previously, once you have begun, you have given inspiration a flow to work with. As you go forward, you may get caught up in the work. When you forget your self-consciousness, something else takes over. You may not be aware of inspiration as it is happening. For inspiration to flow, you have to get out of the way.

Intuition is a direct knowing that comes as sensing or insight. Inspiration is an exalted knowing that brings enthusiasm, excitement, and an enhanced sense of beauty and meaning. Those who have sought inspiration summon a muse, a godlike presence that embodies a beautiful ideal. The lover takes as a muse the entrancing image of the beloved. The favor of inspiration is won by the loving heart. Love of beauty attracts new visions of beauty. The fountain of grace pours upon the uplifted face of those who hunger for beauty and pledge to serve it.

How do you prepare yourself to seek inspiration? Surround yourself with impressions of beauty. There is a theater exercise called extensions, in which you begin by allowing impulse to guide your movement. When the movement flows, you intensify each movement by pushing it to its fullest expression. The intensified movements engage the feelings from which they originated, and those feelings catch on fire. Inspiration arises in the flames of desire, a desire that is fanned by an extension of longing for beauty. Hold before you the vision of the muse, and let your heart stretch toward that uplifting ideal. This is the feeling state that can summon the flow of inspiration.

THOUGHT

THOUGHTS, my constant companions, when do you ever leave me alone?

The moment we try to sit quietly and relax into a silence, we become aware of the continual chatter of the mind. Thoughts can be driven by the endless demands of our everyday responsibilities. They can arise from unresolved emotional experiences, processing relationships, for example. They can be triggered by the body's complaints. Or thoughts can be the processing of impressions from a film, a piece of music, or something read or heard. Thoughts have an annoying persistence when we want some moments of peace.

We tend to regard thoughts as idle activity, not involving exertion, not expending energy. However, the exhaustion that follows stressful thoughts and feelings indicates otherwise. As we saw earlier, a balance of activity and repose includes finding ways to rest the mind, to give it a break from the demanding thought-stream.

In the East, children learn to practice concentrating the mind. That means learning how to hold the mind steady. It has become a cliché that Westerners have a short attention span. Concentration develops the capacity to extend the attention span. Not only does this strengthen your ability to solve problems and be creative, but it also contributes to mental relaxation; because when the mind completes a task, the satisfaction that follows relaxes the mind.

You can practice concentration simply by holding your gaze steadily focused on an object. Choosing a pleasant object to gaze at, also makes a relaxing impression on the mind. Doing this for short periods of time, like five to ten minutes a day, gradually produces perceptible improvement.

Another way to develop concentration is to complete whatever task you take up, even if a better one comes along. After a while, finishing tasks becomes a habit; and the satisfaction, even with small tasks, brings a subtle sense of order and peace.

Where do thoughts come from and where do they go? We may be able to trace many thoughts to specific stimuli, some of which I mentioned earlier. But there are many novel thoughts, intuitions, and inspirations that seem to come from nowhere. We can't trace their origin to ideas from others. Some may arise from associations stimulated by an impression. We might see a flower, for example, and its properties suggest an answer to a problem we've been wrestling with. These kinds of thoughts seem like gifts. Some attribute them to the unconscious or a collective unconscious. Some believe they have a spiritual origin.

The question of *where do they go?* potentially has more serious implications. Mystics believe that thoughts have a life of their own. We may be done with them, but, according to the mystics, they continue on the arc of their intention like arrows released from a bow. If the thought is a wish for some good to happen, the thought continues working in that direction. If the thought is destructive, it goes on with that intention.

The strength of the thought depends on the power of the emotion behind it.

If this is so, then we have a greater responsibility for our thoughts than we might have imagined. We might think that by keeping a rage-filled reaction to ourselves, we have avoided hurting another person. Yes, the overt expression of anger would have obvious consequences. But there could be unseen insidious consequences from the unconscious launching of harsh thoughts.

What can you do about this? Besides doing the psychological work on yourself to reduce the likelihood of an intense reaction, an immediate thing you can do, as soon as you become aware of your reaction and are able to master it, is to send out a counter-thought, a thought of healing and kindness. Any damage done by the first thought can be ameliorated by the blessing of the second.

If you believe that thoughts have a life of their own, then you awaken to your responsibility to be vigilant about your private thoughts and feelings.

RIGHT ASPIRATION

BEFORE embarking on a goal, consider it through a moral lens. What code of morality will you consult? You may believe in a morality inherited from family or church or school. Or maybe your sense of a moral code is vague. You may not have given it much attention.

What are your values? I believe that every person has an innate sense of values. You discover your values by noticing what is important to you. Justice may be a primary value, and also compassion. How these two are balanced for each person may be different. When a judgment is needed, consult your heart to see what feels right. Will the action bring happiness to you and to others or will it bring unhappiness?

It is easy to confuse pleasure with happiness. Pleasure may bring a fleeting happiness followed by distress or regret. True happiness is enduring. When you do the right thing, you feel the peace of real happiness.

What are the implications of the goal you have chosen? Can you foresee unintended consequences? There are always trade-offs in taking any action. By taking one path, other possible paths have to be sacrificed. Dedicating your time and energy in one direction means that it is not available for other possibilities in life. There is no end to possible demands on your time. Everything is calling to us, *what about me?* We can try

124

to respond to all the needs around us and be their servant, or we can take charge and make a commitment to what feels like it is ours to do. This might entail some difficult decisions. When is it right to say no, and when must you sacrifice your goal for the sake of an unavoidable responsibility? These decisions can only be made by letting them sit in the heart and listening to what feels right.

Albert Einstein gave deep consideration to his conscience in dedicating himself to his life work:

> What an extraordinary situation is that of us mortals! Each of us is here for a brief sojourn; for what purpose he knows not, though sometimes he thinks he feels it. But from the point of view of daily life; without going deeper, we exist for our fellow men — in the first place for those on whose smiles and welfare all our happiness depends, and next for all those unknown to us personally with whose destinies we are bound up by the tie of sympathy. A hundred times every day I remind myself that my inner and outer life depend on the labors of other men, living and dead, and that I must exert myself in order to give in the same measure as I have received and am still receiving.[1]

When you have chosen a goal that feels honorable and appears to promise happiness for you and others who will be affected by it, you can proceed with a free conscience.

Living up to your ideal is a continual challenge in life. An inspiring goal can be intoxicating. When following your principles means sacrificing an advantage in moving forward with your goal, it is tempting to compromise, to cut corners. However, being true to

1 Albert Einstein, "The World as I See It" *Forum and Century,* 84: 193–94.

your values is part of the process of fulfilling your purpose. More important than accomplishing the goal, is the manner in which you seek it. Knowing your purpose and working toward it, is changing you, bringing out latent talents and the nobility of your soul. If you lower your standards in order to more easily meet your goal, you are defeating the purpose of having a purpose. The spirit seeks to know itself through your experience. If the limited self distorts the experience for its meager advantage, a great deal is lost; the point of the whole process is compromised. Upholding your values, regardless of the consequences, is not only for the sake of your own fulfillment, but also serves the intelligence that is expressing itself through you.

Emptiness

We are strivers. We are on the go, always trying to do more or to be more. We feel we are not doing enough. Darkness threatens us when we feel we are not doing or being enough.

If we practice silence or meditation, that threat of not being enough might emerge as a feeling of emptiness, as though there is a gaping hole at the center of our being, a vacuum that threatens to swallow us. The feeling of emptiness could seem alien, uncaring, impersonal. We could experience it as a magnetic pull that tugs at our insecure grip on reality.

There is a story of a Zen monk who pours a cup of tea for his student. When the cup is full, he continues to pour as the tea runs over the edge. The monk is giving a message. If your cup is full, there is no room to pour in the teachings. The student needs to bring an empty cup ready to receive. This story refers to the unlearning previously discussed. But the emptiness it speaks of also means a receptive attitude, a state of suspended mental activity. Emptiness is a state of rest, of peace, of openness and trust.

When learning to swim, you first have to overcome your fear of being submerged and drowning. You learn to have confidence in your ability to float.

127

Initially, you may fear drowning in the void of emptiness. Then you learn that you are buoyed up when you let go of your ordinary sense of self. You no longer know who you are, you seem to be without boundaries. Enduring the emptiness, you gain confidence in your ability to float in this condition.

Why bother to pursue emptiness? Because this is the state in which you can receive guidance, knowledge, support, and nurturing from the universal intelligence that gives you life. It is no use trying to control this support. It is freely given but on its own terms. As Jesus says, "Ask and it shall be given."[1] You can pose a question. The answer may not be what you expected; it may not be what you like. But having sought guidance, if you wish to keep up the relationship, it is best to follow the guidance that is given.

Emptiness might seem to be a barren void, but in reality it is just the opposite, a pregnant seedbed of possibility.

---

1 Matthew 7:7.

Part III

Bloom!

Introduction

It is time to turn a corner. So far, the effort to discover a purpose and prepare to enact it has all been directed inward. Of course, our usual habit is to focus our attention outwardly. Generally, our inner life tends to be a reaction to outer experience. In the first two parts of this book, we have explored a proactive orientation to inner experience. We have turned to it for guidance and inspiration. We have sought a vision of our purpose from the mysterious realm of intuition. That vision is the child of our deepest longing, our creative imagination, and our pragmatic resourcefulness. To arrive at our destination, we will need a road map, a plan that breaks down a long journey into doable steps. We will need to gather the required resources. We may need to learn new skills. We will encounter obstacles that will test our resolve. Both successes and failures can throw us off course.

James Dean, the actor, had a clear vision of what his profession required of him.

> An actor must interpret life, and in order to do so must be willing to accept all the experiences life has to offer. In fact, he must seek out more of life than life puts at his feet. In the short span of his lifetime, an actor must learn all that there is to know, experience all there is to experience, or

approach that state as closely as possible. He must be superhuman in his efforts to store away in the core of his subconscious everything that he might be called upon to use in the expression of his art… To grasp the full significance of life is the actor's duty; to interpret it is his problem; and to express it is his dedication.[1]

While we are shaping and changing the world around us, our efforts are also reshaping us. Our longing keeps our vision before us as a guiding star, yet in the end, the process we go through is of greater value than the goal accomplished. Our longing is the bait that lures us from the murky streambed of confusion and ignorance into the sunlit net of the inquiring intelligence, so that it can see itself more clearly and marvel at its glistening beauty.

Is the goal we have discovered our culminating purpose in life? Once there, do we retire to a beach in Florida for the remainder of our days? A wise Sufi has said that our purpose is like the horizon. As you approach it, it recedes further. There is no end to the depth and mystery of the self-revealing Hidden Treasure. Our journey of discovery can stretch out as far before us as we are willing to pursue it.

---

1 James Dean, "James Dean Quotes" IMDb
http://m.imdb.com/name/nm0000015/quotes.

Making a Plan

Up to this point, I have asked you to put aside the mind in order to consult a deeper source of wisdom and insight in the heart. Now is the time to call the ever eager mind into play. It is well suited to the task of making a step-by-step plan.

The distant goal may seem daunting. Once the journey is broken down into steps, put aside any worries about how large the task may seem. Concentrate on the step at hand, trusting that, as you proceed, you will get the help you need. If you are not sure how you will accomplish the next step, if you have resistance or misgivings, step forward, do your best, and persist through failures. Take the failures as opportunities to learn. Keep moving forward to engage the creative flow and the unseen help.

Once you have a plan and have made a commitment to your vision, it is inevitable that life's demands will intervene. How do you spend your time? If you have habits you wish to break, now is the time to practice mastery over those impulses, for the sake of protecting time and energy you wish to dedicate to your goal.

You have a myriad of responsibilities for maintaining the objects you possess. You have social and professional responsibilities. Where can you say no? How can you simplify your life and keep your main focus on what is most important to you?

There are responsibilities that you must honor. When an unexpected duty arises that you can't refuse, what can you do with the conflict that ensues? How can you resolve the commitment to your vision with your sense of duty to family, friends, community, workplace, nation, and the world? But what if these competing demands were actually harmonious with your purpose? What if giving your full attention to another's needs would be helping you with your goal? Can you broaden your view of the journey toward the goal to include everything that happens to you? The plan you draw up may seem to be a straight line to the goal. Imagine the plan as viewing the path with blinders. When the blinders are removed, the straight path is still there, but now a wider view reveals that the digressions leading off from it will enrich the path, strengthening your heart and your faith, and making the straight path easier to follow. You can reduce stress and aggravation by embracing all that comes and seems to take you away from your commitment. See it as a gift that will help you along to eventual fulfillment.

There are three ways of action. You've outlined a plan, gathered the resources you will need, and prepared yourself physically, emotionally, and spiritually. How will you go forward toward your goal?

Consider three temperaments, each with its own way of proceeding.

The first is active, disciplined, and resolute. The active temperament takes the straightforward approach. Take up the first step, do what is required, face problems as they arise and overcome them, and move on through each step in the same way. Though it sounds simple, this way of taking action requires mastery. Self-control is needed to act proactively rather than reacting to unforeseen problems. When an obstacle arises, the actor faces it head-on and seeks a solution. If the first attempt doesn't work, the actor keeps on trying until a solution is found. This person loves a challenge because it brings out the best in him or her. The actor brings will power to bear and sticks to the plan, accomplishing the goal against all odds.

There is another kind of person who welcomes obstacles not as hurdles to overcome but as an integral part of the journey. Everything and every occurrence speaks to the person who has a receptive temperament. The linear plan is an initial path that soon leads out into the expanse of a wider field of play. The planning mind cannot capture the interactive evolution of the path. For the responder, taking a step in the plan is a dialog with a responsive environment. Whatever you experience, there is a message being given. If you encounter an obstacle, it may mean taking a new direction. You flow with the current. The keynote of this approach is faith and surrender. You trust that you are being led toward your goal and welcome every experience along the way as guidance to be digested. Your wish draws the object toward you. The way it comes may be mysterious and serendipitous. You move forward responsively, sensitive to every influence. Accomplishing your goal is a natural unfoldment of a living process.

Jody Williams won a Nobel Prize in 1997 as an activist working to ban land mines. The way she arrived at this work led through many stages and is a good example of the responder.

> Like many of my generation, the Vietnam War
> was a defining experience for me, one that made

me question authority and begin to understand the conflicts between U.S. 'ideals' and its policies that often fly in the face of those ideals.

. . . I lived in Mexico and taught English as a second language. That experience gave me a new understanding of class differences, with gross disparities between the rich and the poor, which so often are root causes of armed conflict.

A couple of years later, these experiences came together in a single moment [when] . . . . I was handed a leaflet entitled, "El Salvador: Another Vietnam?" It resonated with me instantly and deeply — deeply enough that I went to a meeting in a church basement to learn about the wars in Central America . . . And the passion of doing what I considered to be the right thing captured me, and I've never looked back. I worked for over a decade to stop the wars in Central America. I was still doing it when I was asked to help launch the land mine campaign.[1]

The third temperament feels a call to serve others. For the server, the principal factor is balancing the tendencies of the actor and the responder. Sometimes the server proceeds by calling upon mastery, like the actor, and making a mark on the world. In another situation the server may call on faith and flow with the current of the moment, like the responder. No doubt, everyone experiences a blend of mastery and receptiveness. However, for many, one or the other style predominates. For the server, being ambidextrous, the situation calls forth one style or the other.

The server must sometimes overcome injustice or respond to urgent need. This calls for the kind of backbone and courage inherent in the masterful approach.

---

1 Misiroglu, *Imagine*, 108.

To inspire hope, you sometimes have to stand up against the resistance and inertia of rigidified convention.

Toward those you serve, however, you wish to turn a different face, a smiling face of compassion and receptivity. Helping others to achieve greater freedom from circumstances, the server models faith rather than control.

For the server, the challenge is to discriminate when mastery is appropriate and when receptivity is called for.

By getting to know your style, you can avoid feeling pressured by the style or advice of others to act against your nature. Following your style more consciously and deliberately is like practicing a skill. Over time, you develop more facility; and when an obstacle arises, you know how to proceed.

Overcoming Obstacles

ON paper, the plan may look relatively simple and straightforward. Your attitude has much to do with how easily you accomplish each step. It is commonly accepted in sports that success depends on keeping a positive attitude, regardless of how well one is doing. With a keen focus on the immediate challenge and a steel-like determination to do one's best, many setbacks have been overcome, many victories snatched from the jaws of defeat.

I'm ready to go forward. I'm full of enthusiasm and eager to make progress with my plan. I take a few steps and run into a wall. There is no easy way to overcome the obstacle. As one solution after another fails, I get swept up in frustration. Frustration turns to anger, and when I can't overpower the obstacle, I feel I might as well give up.

I am caught in the reactions of my limited self. If I can't get my way, I fume and then feel powerless. I have pitted my self-concept against the world at large, trying to create change. When the world resists, I experience how large it is and how small my poor self is. But let's remind ourselves that the little self that is so easily defeated is only a concept. The true self is unlimited and perfect. How can I recover my equilibrium and make use of this realization?

First, I notice that I am reacting. My reaction is natural. But if I catch myself, I don't have to react. At the moment when I catch myself, I can either let the reaction happen or I can stop it and consider what other options I have. Having decided to stop the reaction, I am free to act instead of reacting. I can deliberately raise my consciousness. I raise it by remembering that I am a human instrument for something much larger and pristine. The spirit that gives me life doesn't have the historical baggage of a self-concept. It is spontaneous, creative, and alive in each moment. When I raise my awareness to this expanded state, I become aware of its integrity and nobility. I don't take a defeat personally; I don't take it as a proof of my shortcomings. I take it calmly and objectively as a problem to be solved.

What can I do with the negative energy that grips me in the form of frustration or anger? If I try to suppress it or deny it, I will find it indigestible. It needs to express itself. Rejected, it lodges itself in the body and psyche as stress. Instead I can sublimate the energy. I move it up from the gut into the heart, and there I can use it for concentration and determination. If I need to express it physically, I can walk or run or put it into some kind of constructive exertion.

Having risen above my reaction, I am back on track to find a creative solution. If my tendency is to take charge and master situations, and if I have tried all the possible solutions I can think of, the next step is to empty the mind, to relax, and entrust the problem to intuition. I pose a question about how to proceed, I rest the mind, sit quietly in suspense, and wait for a dream-like clue. When an impression registers, even if it seems irrelevant, I pay attention and watch it unfold. When it has had a chance to develop, I ask myself what is it saying about my question. If the answer is unclear,

I go back to the first step and try again. When I get a novel solution to the problem, I take a moment to be thankful. Then I make a commitment to carrying it out.

The actor faces the problem head-on and applies will power until the problem is solved. In rising to the test, the actor expects to uncover abilities that have, perhaps, been latent.

The responsive person treats the obstacle as a stubborn and resistant opponent. To make peace with my opponent, first I need to listen carefully to what the opponent is saying. If I can get the message clearly, I will know how to respond. By meeting the need of my opponent, not only will a door open, but I will also gain support to carry me further. My opponent is actually my friend and has something to teach me.

For the balanced temperament there is a choice to make. Does a difficulty call for a masterful approach or a responsive one? Does it need control or trust? What role do I play in the situation? Relationship calls for consideration and respect. How will a response of mastery affect those I wish to serve? If I flow with the situation and trust that it is guiding me, will I be neglecting my responsibility toward those I wish to serve?

There is no right way for all. There is a way that feels right for you. When you find that way, you will feel empowered and at peace.

THE WORD "GOD"

I have deliberately not used the word *God* in this book, because it has complicated associations for Westerners. For some, the notion of God is sacred and the center of their faith. But many have become alienated from Judeo-Christian roots and reject the notion of a distant judging God, who condemns to eternal damnation those who do not faithfully perform stipulated rituals; or who don't accept God's existence on the authority of a church. Some feel that the God of historical religions can be explained as a myth, and turn to science as the only reliable source of truth. Some are drawn to Eastern religions, to Yoga and Buddhism, and find there different notions of God or the absence of God.

It seems to be inherent in the human spirit to seek knowledge, meaning, and sacredness. The Sufi master Pir Vilayat Inayat Khan said that today souls are starving for sacredness. It is missing from our daily lives. How can we bring it back into life?

Belief in God can in most cases be traced back to reverence for a beloved, inspiring prophetic figure like Jesus, Moses, Abraham, Muhammad, Buddha, Rama, Krishna, or Shiva. In Buddhism, sacredness is found not in a notion of God, but in liberation from a narrow point of view. But can you believe in God or liberation without

141

having an actual experience? For some such an experience may come spontaneously. When it comes, its reality can't be denied. It disarms the skeptical mind.

The uncertain mind may think that it must wait for a demonstration of a deeper truth. But there is a proactive alternative. The Sufis say that it is the responsibility of every person to create one's own notion of God. It is a notion that no one can give you. To be genuine, it must come from you. You discover it by noticing what you admire. You pay attention to what you value, what moves you; and you combine those qualities into a vision of an ideal. Once we have a sense of our ideal, we can carry it with us wherever we go. By remembering it and imagining it as beautifully and movingly as we can, we may begin to fall in love with it. The more we keep it with us, the more we begin to experience it as a presence. We need never feel lonely once this presence becomes real.

According to myth, the sculptor Pygmalion becomes entranced with the image of a beautiful woman that he is sculpting. Forgetting any thought of his own limitation, his mind is filled only with his ideal of beauty. The statue he calls *Galatea* exceeds his imagination, and he falls in love with it. His prayers to Aphrodite are answered, and Galatea, his ideal, comes to life.

As an artist, Pygmalion had the skill to shape stone into an image of his ideal of beauty. Where did that ideal come from? It was innate in his imagination. Though most do not have the artistic talent of a Pygmalion, everyone has the innate sense of an ideal. If we consult our imagination, we will find already there those beautiful qualities that most inspire us. Some combination of qualities such as mercy and compassion, kindness, honesty, courage, wisdom, justice, grace, endurance, generosity, love, humor, wit, and many others may be the ingredients of your ideal. It is difficult to hold an ideal image as an abstraction of qualities. Like Pygmalion, envisioning the ideal as a beautiful human being is easier.

Why go to the trouble of bringing one's innate ideal to life? Though we may begin to believe that our presumed self is an illusion, and that there is a true self we can call upon that is much more capable, our preoccupation with our wounds and limitations is difficult to surrender. Our whole life has accustomed us to identify with a socially constructed self. If we are to step out of this identification, we need another place to stand. By shifting our focus from the drama of our personal story to the presence of our beloved Galatea, we can more easily break the old patterns and change our point of view and our attitude toward life.

Earlier, we considered the nature of our inner life as a condition of emptiness continually being filled by a universal intelligence. By becoming detached from the turmoil of life, we can imagine seeing life objectively as the Witness. There is great power in this point of view. It is also rather abstract and colorless.

The practice of bringing to life our innate ideal, falling in love with it, and experiencing it as a constant presence, adds vivid color to the process of freeing ourselves from the little self. Now we can imagine that it is not only the desire of Spirit as a perfect intelligence that is behind our desire, but that Spirit takes on the form of our beloved ideal. And as you pursue your goal, the living presence of your ideal is with you every moment and every step of the way.

There is a practice of concentration that can help you get to know your ideal. Take a beautiful object and place it where you can comfortably gaze at it. Hold your gaze steady for twenty minutes, returning your gaze to the object every time you notice that your concentration has lapsed. The key to this practice is that you imagine your eyes are projecting beams of light to the object. You are casting the light of your intelligence onto the object. After twenty minutes, what may happen is that the object seems to open up and reveal its secret. What is its secret? It is a kind of inner radiance and subtle essence.

Something subtle and alive seems to transpire through the appearance of the object.

In the process of thinking more and more about your ideal, something similar can happen. The notion you have created, or better, that you have discovered, opens up and reveals its secret. It comes alive. In the light of this revelation, your everyday or presumed self is eclipsed.

This is the experience of Buddhist liberation, and also the mystic's experience of God. It can't be captured in a notion of God. It is an irreducible experience. The experience of God is self-revealing. It responds to your effort to know yourself. By becoming familiar with your particular inherent ideal, you are coming to know yourself at a deep level. It is natural that your heart is stirred by witnessing your ideal. Then love arises, and your presumed self begins to long for the ideal. The power of love, which shines through your ardent glance, attracts the Beloved. The Beloved wishes to reveal the Beloved's own Self, but will only respond to a heart burning with love. Once you have been embraced by the subtle essence of love, then the questions, *Does God exist? and if so, what notion of God is right?* seem irrelevant. Instead, you feel that *wherever I turn my face, there is the face of God*. Whatever God is, God is everywhere, in everything. There is nothing that is without God.

INTEGRATION

THE language of duality, our usual way of under-standing things, attempts to deal with the phenome-non of unity when it reaches an impasse. I have spoken of God as the revelation of an inner ideal, which comes to life in the guise of a Beloved. And I have introduced the idea of a Hidden Treasure that seeks to know itself through our experience, as we discover our purpose and unfold our hidden strengths in the process of pur-suing it. Then again, there is the notion of the Witness, pure intelligence that sees through our eyes and is our true natural self, free of self-concepts. How does this all fit together?

Our presumed self, our usual sense of identity, is so firmly fixed in our imagination, that we will get the most benefit from these points of view by seeing how they can be incorporated into daily life. We can become more objective about our limitations and our life path by stepping outside our usual identity from time to time, and seeing ourselves through the eyes of the compassionate and nurturing Witness. With objectivity, we can hope for greater clarity and insight. Gradually, we can hope to release ourselves from the grip of self-absorption and the neuroses stemming from ques-tions of self-worth.

Try to imagine that a greater purpose lies behind your individual purpose, and that there is a powerful hand helping you along and rooting for your success. The notion of the Hidden Treasure reminds us that we are not alone in our pursuit. Our purpose has meaning as part of the whole purpose. We are sounding our note in the symphony of the whole. Those magical moments in childhood when the world was new can be revived when we discover that the secrets of the Hidden Treasure are endless. There is wonder in the realization that we are playing a part in a greater self-discovery, so to speak: the universe becoming aware of itself.

When you are engaged in discovering your ideal being and making it a real presence by holding it before you, it leaves its impression on your personality. It influences the way you behave and awakens appreciation and thankfulness. It opens your eyes to see beauty and harmony in life, where before you may have missed it. Basic trust in life and in yourself increases, and this makes accomplishing your goal easier.

So the pure intelligence of the Witness, the Hidden Treasure wishing to be known, and the Beloved who reveals the Beloved's own Self through your ideal, are they all one and the same? From the point of view of unity, yes they are the same. Everything is of the same essence. From the point of view of duality, we may experience these aspects of unity as different. It might be helpful to imagine that they arise from a common root. To this picture we need to add everything else; all stem from the same root.

Prayer

We humans build relationships by communication. Conversation, presence, touch, and shared activity develop intimacy. Holding a vision of your ideal is a step toward building a relationship between your everyday self and the essential self. From the point of view of the limited self, the essential self is experienced as the Guide or the Guardian. Prayer serves as a way to bring intimacy to this relationship.

In childhood, we are dependent on our parents or caregivers. As we mature we are weaned and are expected to become self-reliant. Self-reliance is a cultural ideal. It hurts our pride when we must depend on others. In our relationships it is embarrassing to ask a favor of another. We would rather be the giver than the receiver.

With the Guardian, we can be like children, simple and trusting. In humility we can ask for help as Jesus advised, "Ask and it shall be given."[1] If we have doubt, however, the asking turns into a test. If we ask and nothing seems to happen, we may feel our doubts are justified, or we may feel unworthy and abandoned. What if we affirmed that our ideal Guardian is benevolent and wishes for our success? If we are ready to put ourselves fully into the hands of a greater reality, releasing outmoded ideas of a judging, critical, condemning

1 Matthew 7:7.

God, then we can open up and relax. We will have patience for the outcome of our prayer, which may come in unexpected ways.

When we can't see the way forward, we can release tension and doubt, and learn to rely on inner help. We can bring the vision of our inherent ideal to life through prayer in its aspects of conversation, shared activity, and intimate presence.

Prayer also serves as a reminder to keep awake, to remember our true nature in the midst of so many stimuli that reinforce our limited self-concept. It is difficult to hold on to an abstract notion of an unlimited source underlying our presumed self, when life is continually tugging us away from this realization. Prayer helps to bring this influence concretely into life by linking our everyday experience with our realization of something larger and higher. It is a reminder that a hidden power is working behind our wish, bringing it to fruition.

Pir Vilayat Inayat Khan has said that prayer is the most creative of acts. How is it creative? How do we experience creativity? It seems to come from elsewhere as a gift. It comes as a flow. A flow must come through a channel. If the channel is blocked, the flow becomes congested, and there is strain. When the weight of responsibility falls on the small self, and it feels that it must act with self-reliance, the small self may feel crushed. It may shut down. The channel may become blocked. What blocks the free flow of creativity is preoccupation with the little self. When the presumed self puts itself wholly into the arms of the Guardian like a trusting child, consciousness becomes focused on the unlimited ideal. This opens your receptive capacity and creativity can flow unobstructed. The hidden richness that is your heritage is waiting to be called on. It can't make its way through a cramped and congested passageway. Relaxing the pride of self-reliance, allowing yourself to feel the humility of childhood, and opening yourself with trust to the help of a loving presence allows the creative juices to flow. Prayer builds a collaborative relationship between the presumed self, functioning in the world, and its root source.

SUSTAINING THE EFFORT

AN effort that begins with great enthusiasm, with a bright vision and high hopes, can gradually lose steam. Besides the unexpected obstacles that have to be overcome or circumvented, inspired visions often require a considerable amount of mundane routine work. Even inspiring work can become a chore when inspiration is required day after day. The burst of energy released in taking the first steps can dwindle simply because it can't be sustained, physically and emotionally.

How can you manage your psychic and emotional resources to make the journey easier? When we feel motivated and excited, our reaction is to launch ahead, without much thought of pacing ourselves. And when we feel exhausted, our reaction tends to be to feel discouraged and lose interest. Seeing that we are committing ourselves for the long run, we can anticipate these extremes by practicing balance. For every effort put forth, we need to counter it with a period of rest. When we are riding the crest of the wave of creativity, can we step back, confident that the creative flow will be there when we return? And when we feel tired and our interest is waning, can we dive back into the wave and find our bearings again?

The overall approach to the goal is divided into two parts: on the one hand, intuition, vision, and the plan;

and, on the other hand, action and completion of the task. The first part is receptive and inward, and the second part is expressive and active. You call upon intuition and guidance in the first part, and intention and will in the second.

There is an art to balancing these two modes of working once you have started to carry out the plan. Too much action and too much will push the project forward, but lack thought and consideration. Too much caution, trying to anticipate all the possible ramifications of action, holds back the action. The ideal would be to find balance in a rhythmic way: now going forward, and now reviewing the progress and considering consequences and improvements.

When interest wanes, there is a danger of being tempted to switch the goal to something else which looks more appealing. If you fail to complete the goal there are consequences for your self-confidence. Steadiness with the goal you have chosen for the sake of building your strength through success, overrides the need to be motivated in the moment. Here is where mastery over impulse plays a vital role in keeping the ship on course.

There is another consideration. By seeking a goal deeply inside and making a commitment to it, you are unleashing a living process. You have enlisted a hidden power to stand behind you and support your intention. As long as you are engaged in the process, it goes along the track of your intention. But if you abandon it, it continues onward blindly, without a dedicated instrument. It is like a genie (the powerful spirit freed from the bottle that serves your wish) run amok. And the original intention, without piloting, can become distorted and destructive. Once you have launched a committed effort, you have a responsibility to care for it and lead it safely into port. As long as you are in charge, you can call on the power of the genie to ensure a safe journey.

SACRIFICE

WHEN a young person moves out of the childhood home, there is a period of newfound freedom to explore life. If that person has no responsibility for others, then the field is wide open for new experiences. Life is fresh and new for a while. Unless there is a clear direction, eventually the novelty gets stale. Everything changes when you fall in love. For the sake of your partner, you are willing to sacrifice some of your freedoms. The warmth and trust you find in the relationship is worth more than the passing pleasures you may have become accustomed to.

Pursuing your purpose also calls for sacrifice. Without love for what you wish to accomplish and for the process of doing it, you will make sacrifices reluctantly. Be clear about what is important to you. Remember that you are lending yourself to a larger will. Are you being considerate to the intention that stands behind your wish? Are you showing up or tarrying on the way?

How do you decide when to sacrifice? You will need to call on intuitive wisdom to help sort out this complex judgment. As noted before, there are responsibilities we can't ignore. Making a sacrifice in such a case would be selfish. In part, your commitment to your purpose is a pledge to keep your heart open. Anything that closes the heart, though it might appear to be in service to the goal, is working against your purpose. If saying no means closing your heart, trying to uphold your commitment could be self-defeating.

But not every such case is clear. Where do you draw the line? There will be many demands on your time and energy. Sometimes it is right to say no. Only you can say where the boundary lies. You will have to consult your inner wisdom for each case.

It is easier to identify those temptations that have become comfortable habits. Giving up your comforts is not easy, especially when the path has become thorny or you are struggling with weariness. Sometimes giving in to something comforting can help relieve a stagnating effort. When you choose to do something comforting, be sure to take a break intentionally and thoroughly enjoy it. Cultivate new ways to renew your spirit such as appreciating the beauty of nature or relaxing in silence and feeling the peace and light in your inner life.

Comforting habits, however, can be subtly addictive. Once you make a resolution to change, you discover how tightly the habit clings to its life. Though your intention is clear, the temptation keeps reasserting itself, especially in weaker moments. It takes patience and determination to break free. The Buddhist practice of simple awareness, catching myself at the moment when I am tempted, and observing myself objectively, has helped me gradually break long-standing habits. Falling into self-judgment and remorse only feeds energy into the struggle. Forgiving myself, leaving the past behind, and focusing on renewed effort is more effective.

Why sacrifice present pleasure for an uncertain future reward? Pleasures of the moment are passing. They

154

have no lasting value. They lead nowhere. They may later feel like time wasted or, worse, they may have destructive consequences.

Taking up what is meaningful to you, unfolding the person you are meant to be, discovering and honing your innate talents, is far more rewarding than enjoying the comforting pleasure of the moment. Much of the time, the pursuit of purpose will not feel comforting. It will be challenging, frustrating, and discouraging. It will require will power to overcome lethargy and resistance.

Becoming acquainted with sacrifice at first is difficult. After the first victories, the value of sacrifice becomes more evident. The experience is similar to what happens when you practice mastery. Success gives you a feeling of satisfaction and strength. With greater confidence, the challenge becomes easier. As you progress you are able to sacrifice more and more pebbles for pearls. You are tailoring your life to serve a larger purpose. Though commitment to purpose is not easy, in the long run it brings you happiness and peace.

SUCCESS

SUCCESS can be intoxicating. But our self-confidence is fragile. It is easier for us to see our faults and limitations than to believe in our strengths. We are hungry for reassurance and appreciation. If success goes to your head, you may not handle it well. With pride cometh a fall, and the benefit of success is spoiled.

It is the preoccupation with our self-concept, trying to shore it up against self-doubts, that gets us into trouble. Remind yourself that your self-concept is only a concept. What is real and enduring is the mysterious stream of life and intelligence that animates it. Taking pride in your self is perilous, but taking pride in the universal intelligence as the source of your success builds confidence in that inner resource. To promote humility in your limited self, can you make a point of acknowledging and feeling thankful for the support of unseen help?

A public success carries with it the discomfort of raised expectations. Can you repeat the success or was it only a lucky fluke? One would hope for a gradual maturing and refining of one's gifts, with success building on success. But insecurity can undermine this natural unfoldment.

If you judge a success as a flash in the pan, a burst of naive enthusiasm and novelty, then you can become the slave of your success. On the other hand, if you see success as a gift from the unseen, as a deep impersonal wish expressing itself through your desire, then, in humility, you can go on improving yourself as an instrument, trusting that as long as your desire is alive, the underlying wish in its quest for perfection will go on finding new successes.

Failure along the way is inevitable. Embrace failure as a steppingstone toward success. Success is meant to foster success. The right placement of pride and humility, freeing yourself from the turmoil of the presumed self, will keep the ship heading in the right direction.

As you gain confidence in the inner impulse, you can gradually wean yourself from the influence of the approbation or criticism coming from others. Instead of reacting to the judgment of others, you begin to care less about honors or disapproval. What is the real meaning of success? It is a feeling of peace and relaxation in your innards, a feeling that I have accomplished what I have felt called to do, no matter what others may think of it.

There are many stories of pioneers in art, science, and social reform who broke old conventions. They persisted in their visions in spite of rejection and, often, hostility toward their contributions. The strength of their belief in what was coming through them overcame their personal need for approval. Viewed from the lens of a limited self, they could be seen as particularly strong egos, and that appraisal might carry a negative judgment. Whatever aspects of strong ego they may have carried, I believe what accounts for their success and enduring contributions is their trust in the inner fire that drove them.

the Cycle of Wish and Will

YOU'VE discovered that you have a great wish, a dream that you hope someday to achieve. You work hard, undergo disappointments, and make sacrifices; and one day it happens. You've achieved it. You celebrate, you feel proud of your accomplishment. And then what? You may be left with a hole in your life, no longer filled by the dream and the struggle. You have what you wished for but, gradually, you begin to take having it for granted. The elusive goal once attained loses its luster. While you were striving for it, you felt strength and meaning in your commitment. Now that you have it, do you become beholden to it? Do you become its servant, no longer in charge of the direction of your life? If you cling to it, you will have to maintain it. Routine may replace inspiration.

There is a rhythm in our lives that we may have overlooked. From our usual point of view, a wish arises from we know not where. If we take it seriously, we devote ourselves to finding a way to accomplish it. We form an intention and exert will power to carry out the steps until we achieve the goal.

Let's look at this process from a larger point of view. Picture a circle with a starting point at the top, a downward arc on the right side and an upward arc on the left side. Imagine that the seed wish underlying your personal wish is released from the top point. It travels down the right arc, entering your awareness and becoming solidified as an intention and a plan. The downward arc represents the wish coming into consciousness and being adopted. When the impulse reaches the bottom, the will takes over and actualizes the wish, bringing it to life in the material world. The process of actualizing it occupies the left upward arc. When the impulse reaches the top again the goal is achieved. The cycle is complete. The seed wish issuing from the pure intelligence or Hidden Treasure has found its instrument and has become materialized.

Now recall the Sufi idea that the purpose is like the horizon, ever receding. Once you have reached the apparent horizon, you will see a further horizon beyond. The natural next step, having completed the cycle of manifesting a seed wish, is to start a new cycle. As a contemporary Sufi master put it, you leap from the top of one cycle to the top of the next. In other words, you start the process over again.

Having come all this way, through struggles and perils, and having finally reached the goal and savored victory, it is not so easy to turn away from your hard-won success and start again at the very beginning. You would like to bask for a while in the glory of achievement. But we know that the satisfaction of the false self is short-lived.

Much more valuable is the faith and strength that you have gained. More important is the fire of longing lit by the next wish, and the hope for a further achievement that motivates and inspires.

Whatever you have accomplished has prepared you for the next goal that will be larger and more challenging. The pursuit of your purpose is making you larger and more capable. It is improving the instrument through which the spirit plays its song. Your note is being sounded with greater strength and purity.

THE PROCESS RATHER THAN THE GOAL

In late nineteenth-century India, classical musicians sought their fortunes in the courts of the maharajas. Success in their profession depended on the patronage of a maharaja.

A young, highly gifted musician was just setting out on a new career and was as yet unknown. He decided to seek the patronage of the Nizam of Hyderabad, the foremost patron of the arts in India at that time. His first step was to ask his friends to help him secure an audition. They scoffed at his audacity. The greatest artists of India performed at the court of the Nizam. It would be presumptuous for an unknown musician taking the first step in his career to apply to this court.

So the young man decided to pray and put all his trust in Providence. He rented a room in Hyderabad, and spent his days praying and practicing. Many months passed, but he held firmly to his faith.

One day a friend came to visit and mentioned that he had been invited to visit the prime minister of Hyderabad. He asked the young man if he would like to join him. The prime minister happened to be out of favor with the Nizam and was looking for some way to please him. When he found out that the young man was an accomplished musician, he wondered if this was his opportunity. As fate would have it, the Nizam

161

was returning from a journey, and sent word ahead that he wished to visit the home of the prime minister that very night.

When the Nizam arrived, the prime minister introduced the young man and offered to have him play for the entourage. The Nizam enjoyed the music so much that he encouraged him to continue playing for several hours. At the end of the recital, the Nizam honored him with the title Tansen of India, comparing him with one of India's greatest musicians.

In that moment, the young man had achieved his impossible goal. Yet to him this honor and great achievement meant nothing compared with what he had learned about the power of depending solely on faith.

The process proved to be greater than achieving the success.

The picture that I presented early in this book was a simplified linear process, in which the universal intelligence or Hidden Treasure sparks a seed wish in you, with the limited self as its instrument, and comes to know itself through your experience of unfolding latent gifts and strengths. Opening the heart and expanding the capacity to love also plays a part in the fulfillment of this process.

Such a picture is useful in shifting your attitude toward yourself and the meaning of life. Of course, the reality is vastly more subtle and complex. At this point I would like to add to this picture the element of mutuality.

Rainer Maria Rilke's poem, "The Man Watching," gives a potent image of this mutuality. His metaphor for the mysterious unseen power that works behind the scenes is a driving storm. It is irresistible. Our encounter with it is like Jacob wrestling with an angel.

Whoever was beaten by this Angel
(who often declined to fight)
went away proud and strengthened
and great from that harsh hand,
that kneaded him as if to change his shape.
Winning does not tempt that man.
This is how he grows: by being defeated, decisively,
by constantly greater beings.[1]

While the Hidden Treasure, that immense irresistible power, achieves its aim through our success, we are growing with each successive challenge. Our growth depends on the false self being overpowered by an angel. We go through tests in pursuit of our goal. Without these tests, we wouldn't know what we are capable of. As we grow and take on greater challenges, we find we can do more. Our dependence on our self-concept, which is fettered by limitation, is defeated by a growing realization and dependence on our angel self, the pure essence that animates us and is emitted from a perfect source. With each round in the cycle of attainment, we encounter a greater angel; and our persisting sense of limitation is decisively defeated again, but at a deeper level.

While the unitary consciousness is coming to know itself through the miracle of this glorious manifested world, our little self is expanding, step by step awakening to its true nature. The unknown is moving toward knowing itself, and we are moving toward knowing the unknown.

---

1 Rainer Maria Rilke, *Selected Poems of Rainer Maria Rilke: A Translation from the German and Commentary*, trans. Robert Bly.

AWAKENING

THERE is a famous Taoist story about a Chinese philosopher who dreamed he was a butterfly. When he awoke, he couldn't be sure whether he was a man who dreamed he was a butterfly, or a butterfly who was dreaming that he was a man. We think we can clearly distinguish between being awake and being asleep. We take it for granted that our usual daily state of awareness constitutes what it means to be awake. But what if our usual sense of self is actually a dream, and all these years when we thought we were awake, we were actually dreaming?

It is told in the Islamic tradition that the soul of Adam refused to enter the little prison of clay prepared for it. God commanded the angels to sing. Carried away by the ecstasy of the music, the soul of Adam entered the body, which enabled it to dance.

Mystics of all traditions have taught that the true nature of a human being is much greater than our ordinary self-concept. We have come from a more expansive existence, and we will return to it again when this life ends. Our experience is squeezed down into a very narrow space in this life.

Getting to know your life's purpose, coming to feel at home in the silence, listening to the subtle urgings of inner guidance, experiencing the helping hand behind the scenes, testing yourself and bringing forth latent gifts, all of these things contribute to thinning the clouds of the narrow little self-concept, and to revealing glimpses of the vast sky and brilliant sun that have always been there. Each time your habit of smallness is defeated by a glimpse of a greater reality, you are beginning to awaken from a dark dream.

As long as the ideas in this book are just ideas, you are a person dreaming of being a butterfly. When your attitude shifts, when experience shows you the reality hinted at by these ideas, you discover that you are actually a butterfly that has long dreamed that it was a contrived self. The insecurities of that dream begin to melt in the sunlight. You are awakening to an existence that you can't really define. There is greater clarity and simplicity. You feel more peaceful. You are free of so many bonds that have been constricting you. The beauty of nature is more apparent. You feel tolerant and forgiving of others, seeing the burdens they are carrying. You find that happiness is not something you have to pursue, but is your own nature.

At first, waking up may come in temporary glimpses. If you keep on the path of seeking meaning and purpose, you will be waking yourself up. Gradually, the dream of the soul finding itself imprisoned in a narrow container will fade, and the privilege of being human, of having the opportunity to grow and realize will dawn.

THE PATH OF SADHANA

YOU may have the impression that following a spiritual path means dropping out of the mainstream and joining an exclusive community. Perhaps you imagine that belonging to such a community entails adopting alien customs, clothing, or spiritual exercises. However, the journey of seeking the purpose of your life and growing as a person in the process is a spiritual path that can be followed in the natural course of life. It is a path that is accessible to anyone living in a Western culture, as an extension of everyday life. When you follow this path, you can imagine that your spiritual community consists of those people living ordinary lives who take ideas such as the ones in this book to heart.

The path of attainment is a recognized spiritual path in the East. In the Yoga tradition it is called the path of *sadhana*. As a Yogic path the practice of mastery is generally a personal discipline to accomplish a deep state of meditation. The path of attainment in life described in this book is a Sufi version of sadhana based on the teachings of Hazrat Inayat Khan.

What is a spiritual path, and why would you care whether or not you were following a spiritual path? Following a path means that you have a sense of direction in your life, you are moving toward a destination.

Calling it a spiritual path means that your goal goes beyond material gain. It means that you are choosing to move in a direction that brings greater spirit into your life. It means that you acknowledge there is more to life than the material world has to offer.

Having an intuitive sense that you are being called to do something in life, to sound your note, then seeking the help of spirit, of the unseen, is a natural place to turn. Once you turn to spirit by cultivating an inner life, you are on a spiritual path.

Fulfilling your purpose by accomplishing something meaningful may seem like the ultimate destination of this path of attainment. There is a Sufi saying, "Make God a reality and God will make you the Truth."[1] When you serve the seed wish of spirit and make that wish a reality, you are also making spirit a reality. You are bringing about the materialization of spirit. The echo of this phenomenon is the spiritualization of matter. There is a mutuality, an exchange, in the act of communion with spirit. When you willingly accept the role of instrument for spirit, your sense of self gets transformed. It is raised to a higher octave. When the presence of the helping spirit becomes real for you, you become more real. Your everyday self becomes more authentic. Your integrity is enhanced. The purpose of your life is not only to achieve a goal, or to advance toward the horizon of successive goals. The path of attainment leads to awakening and transformation.

---

1 Inayat Khan, *The Complete Sayings of Hazrat Inayat Khan*, 6.

COLLECTIVE AWAKENING

AWAKENING is a natural process. It can happen by following the path of attainment as described in this book. There are many other ways it can happen as well.

Hazrat Inayat Khan believed that, just as an individual passes through stages of development with new capabilities arising with each further step, humanity as a whole has developed and gained new capacities over the centuries. He saw the time coming when human consciousness will be ready for a collective awakening.

According to his vision, when that time comes, the unity underlying the appearance of diversity will become apparent to many. Individuals will recognize not only their own connection to a vast and mysterious spirit or pure intelligence, but will also realize that the same spirit is present in every other person, regardless of nationality, ethnicity, gender, personality, or eccentricity.

On that basis, fear and distrust will fade, tolerance will grow, old wounds will heal, and long-estranged brothers and sisters will settle their differences and reunite in a single human family.

Imagine the one spirit behind all as an immense oceanic heart. Its tide long ago flowed out, casting its foam and droplets onto distant shores. Now the current is reversed. The pull of its passion is drawing back every precious molecule of water into its loving embrace. The power of unity is even now reversing the terrible isolation and loneliness of souls. The rolling of the tide whispers, *Wake up, wake up, come back to me willingly or be swept up blindly.*

There are many crises facing humanity that portend a grim future. We hope that rationality and human ingenuity can save us from looming disaster. More potent than these hopes is the promise of awakening. Some look for a charismatic savior to lead us to safety. The savior may indeed appear, but this time the savior will be us, a collective savior. Or perhaps it would be better to say that the one savior has always been there. The breakthrough will come when that savior can work through a multitude of willing instruments. When that day arrives, everything will be possible.

Conclusion of Fulfilling
Your Purpose in Life

YOUR life matters. The whole scheme of things remains incomplete if it is missing the part you are meant to play. I don't say this to put pressure on you. Modern life already puts too much of a burden on our shoulders.

The path of attainment is a path to peace and happiness. It is grounded in faith and sustained by mastery. When you discover what you are meant to do, a new joy comes into your life.

It is not an easy path. There are many hardships and sacrifices. But as it progresses, the evidence of the unseen help and support becomes stronger. The burden you carry is made lighter. Your strength and capacity grow.

When you find meaning in your life, it doesn't matter if your path takes you through routine, tedium, or scary new territory. Everything you do is for a worthwhile end. Your life makes sense in a larger context. You are fulfilling a deep seed wish, a wish arising in love. Whether or not you leave a legacy for others, you are satisfying a greater need in the order of things. Like the plant that culminates in a flower and perfume, your bloom is unique and gives delight to the gardener who planted it.

Part IV

THE TREE OF LIFE

INTRODUCTION

here is the deepest secret nobody knows
(here is the root of the root and the bud of the bud
and the sky of the sky of a tree called life; which grows
higher than soul can hope or mind can hide)
and this is the wonder that's keeping the stars apart
i carry your heart (i carry it in my heart)
                                                    —e. e. cummings[1]

So far we have considered sadhana, the path of accomplishment, as the process of achieving something meaningful in the outer life. We have turned to the inner life as a source of inspiration and guidance. We have aspired to free ourselves more and more from the grip of the isolating ego, with its litany of complaints and woes. By a radical acceptance of the necessity of limitations and shortcomings, we can turn around our self-critical insecurities, and see them as opportunities for continual growth toward our innate sense of an ideal.

We have adopted a bifocal vision of ourselves as an instrument of a universal Spirit, while, at the same time being witness and participant in the drama of life.

We see in a tree many stages of maturation. The development of branches, the sprouting of leaves, the

---

1 e. e.cummings, *Complete Poems, 1913–1962* (New York: Harcourt, Brace, and Jovanovich, 1972).

budding of flowers, and ripening of fruit, and finally the production of new seeds. So in the human, there are many stages of maturation. There is the maturation of the body, whose fruit is seen in the beauty and energy of youth. There is the maturation of the mind, which is fulfilled when an independent adult is able to solve problems and function in life. There is the maturation of the heart, when one is freely able to give and receive love. The subject of this book could be termed the maturation of the soul. Its fulfillment is the achievement of one's goal and the flowering of hidden gifts.

As with the tree, each flowering is followed by a fading. The body declines. The keenness of mental pursuits fades. The passion of love mellows. Even the longing that has driven your sense of purpose reaches a stage of world-weariness. This differs from a mood of discouragement. It is not a reaction to feeling defeated in your efforts. Success is yours. But then what? Is this all there is? Having accomplished my purpose in life, am I done? Is life over?

Recall the idea that purpose is like the horizon. When you come close to fulfilling the purpose you know, a further purpose appears on the horizon. To keep the momentum going when you complete one goal, you look for the next goal and start the process over.

World-weariness may come after completing one goal or many goals in your outward life. When it comes, the outer goals no longer appeal. But certain primal universal desires remain. The tree of life has its ultimate blossoming inwardly.

Hazrat Inayat Khan identifies five basic desires whose fulfillment can only be found in the inner life. They are the desire for knowledge, for life, for power, for joy, and for peace. The pursuit of these desires is not just for mystics. It is a natural process, just as all the maturations of the body, mind, heart, and soul unfold by themselves. This further stage could be called maturation of embodied Spirit.

This part of the book takes a look at the process of fulfilling each of these basic desires.

SEEKING TRUTH — DESIRE FOR KNOWLEDGE

WHEN we speak of knowledge, we usually mean an intellectual understanding of how things work. But of course, we have acquired a great deal of knowledge that we take for granted; for example, the knowledge that allows us to speak a language, to read, or to make simple calculations. We have acquired a vocabulary of sounds and smells that we readily recognize. We remember names and identify faces. We possess a vast amount of practical and specialized knowledge that seems mostly ordinary. We are never satisfied with the knowledge we have. We always want to know more. What knowledge will ever satisfy us?

Outer knowledge can give us a clue. The scientist discovering the intricacy and elegance of nature experiences awe and wonder. The artist can be transported by an inner experience of beauty and harmony that can only be approximated, even in works of great genius. The person living close to the earth feels wrapped in its pristine matrix, at home and at one with the flow of life. The lover is moved by the beauty of the beloved's personality. The maker of things revels in the sensations and properties of materials.

Yet always this knowledge is limited. That there is an unlimited knowledge, a knowledge that gives lasting satisfaction, has been claimed by the pioneers at the further reaches of consciousness, in all cultures. Some speak of it in religious language, and others in the language of experience. It is the nature of this truth that what it is cannot be comprehended by the mind, much less expressed in words. What the pioneers have been able to do is point the way one must travel to seek it.

What is the obstacle standing in the way of discovering it? It is the very notion of limitation, our old friend, the presumed self. Can the ocean be poured into a cup? In the Bible it is said that if one came face to face with the Holy of Holies, one would be shattered — the fate of the bottle trying to swallow the ocean.

We seek to possess more and more knowledge, but truth is a knowledge we cannot possess. Through knowledge, we hope to prop up the insecure ego against the many dangers that threaten it. But truth cannot be appropriated by the ego. For the knowledge of truth, what is needed is trusting surrender. Unable to possess the knowledge of truth, we find we need to be possessed by it.

Recall the practice of climbing the ladder of increasingly intensified imagination. You could imagine a brighter and brighter light. As the intensity of concentration increases, you cross a threshold and the light takes over. You are possessed by the light.

Rilke's picture of how we grow in stature is that we are continually defeated by ever greater angels. It is a process in which again and again, the self-assertion of the ego fails, and we open up to being possessed by an ever greater infusion of mysterious grace.

Satisfying the primal desire for knowledge is possible for every soul. There is a spark of passion in us that requires stoking if we are to seek the direct experience of truth.

The poet Rumi says,

> *There is a candle in your heart, ready to be kindled.*
> *There is a void in your soul, ready to be filled.*
> *You feel it, don't you?[1]*

You can become aware of that spark and you can learn how to blow on it. There is a longing in you to go home. All of your earthly homes remind you of it. When you stoke that longing, the flame rises, and in its light, you begin to glimpse the truth.

---

1 Shahram Shiva, *Hush, Don't Say Anything to God: Passionate Poems of Rumi.* (Fremont, CA: Jain Publishing Company, 1999).

Testimony of the Sages

THE search for truth is universal. It is expressed differently in the language of each culture, but the veil of language still reveals the common contours hidden beneath. Rumi, in a few words, describes the preconditions for this search, to go beyond the process of inquiry we are used to and to gain access to a state which is self-revealing. Here are two brief contributions from Rumi:

> *Sell your cleverness and buy bewilderment.*
>
> *At night, I open the window*
> *and ask the moon to come*
> *and press its face against mine.*
> *Breathe into me.*
> *Close the language-door*
> *and open the love-window.*
> *The moon won't use the door,*
> *only the window.*
> *No more words.*[1]

Listen to the instructions of the early Christian thinker Dionysius the Areopagite:

---

1 Rumi, *The Masnavi*, book 4; *Like This*, translated by Coleman Barks (Athens, GA: Maypop, 1990).

Do thou, dear Timothy, in the diligent exercise of mystical contemplation, leave behind the senses and the operations of the intellect, and all things sensible and intellectual, and all things in the world of being and non-being, that thou mayest arise by unknowing towards the union, as far as is attainable, with Him who transcends all being and all knowledge. For by the unceasing and absolute renunciation of thyself and of all things, thou mayest be borne on high, through pure and entire self-abnegation, into the superessential radiance of the divine Darkness.[2]

And similar sentiments we find in the words of Saint Theresa of Avila.

Let (the soul) try, without forcing itself or causing any turmoil, to put a stop to all discursive reasoning, yet not to suspend the understanding, nor to cease from all thought, though it is well for it to remember that it is in God's presence and Who this God is. If feeling this should lead it into a state of absorption, well and good; but it should not try to understand what this state is, because that is a gift bestowed upon the will. The will, then, should be left to enjoy it, and should not labour except for uttering a few loving words, for although in such a case one may not be striving to cease from thought, such cessation often comes, though for a very short time."[3]

The experience of truth is direct, synthetic, and whole, not analytical. The Christian contemplative Nicholas of Cusa, explains what a direct experience of truth is like.

2 *The Mystical Theology and the Celestial Hierarchies of Dionysius the Areopagite* (Goldalming, Surrey, UK: Shrine of Wisdom, 2004), 1.
3 Theresa of Avila, *Interior Castle*, trans. E. Allison Peers (New York: Bantam Doubleday/Dell Publishing Group, 1990), 89–90.

Just as any knowledge of the taste of something we have never actually tasted is quite empty until we do taste it, so the taste of this wisdom cannot be acquired by hearsay, but by one's actually touching it with his internal sense, and then he will bear witness not of what he has heard but what he has experientially tasted in himself. To know of the many descriptions of love which the saints have left us without knowing the taste of love is nothing other than a certain emptiness. Thus it is that it is not enough for him who seeks after eternal wisdom to merely read about these things, but it is absolutely necessary that once he discovers where it is by his understanding he make it his very own.[4]

The Sufi mystic Ibn 'Arabi echoes the idea of a direct experience.

Such knowledge can only be had by actual experience, nor can the reason of man define it, or arrive at any cognizance of it by deduction, just as one cannot, without experience, know the taste of honey, the bitterness of patience, the bliss of sexual union, love, passion, or desire.[5]

The Greek thinker Plotinus, cautions patience. You cannot push to make the experience happen. It has to happen in its own time.

We ought not to question whence it [the experience of Unity] comes; there is no whence, no coming or going in place; it either appears [to us] or does not appear. We must not run after it, but we must fit ourselves for the vision and then wait tranquilly for it as the eye waits on the rising of

---

4 *Unity and Reform Selected Writings of Nicholas of Cusa*, ed. J.P. Dolan (Chicago: University of Notre Dame Press, 1962), 111–12.
5 Muhyi ad-Din Ibn 'Arabi, *The Bezels of Wisdom*, trans. R.W.J. Austin (Mahwah, NJ: Paulist Press, 1980), 25.

the Sun which in its own time appears above the horizon and gives itself to our sight.[6]

The Jewish philosopher Solomon ben Judah emphasizes priming your imagination by painting for yourself the picture of your highest ideal.

> If you wish to form a picture of the [divine] Substance, you must raise your intellect to the last [substance] intelligible. You must purify it from all sordid sensibility, free it from the captivity of nature and approach with the force of your intelligence to the last limit of intelligible substance that it is possible for you to comprehend, until you are entirely divorced from sensible substance and lose all knowledge thereof. Then you will embrace, so to speak, the whole corporeal world in your being, and will place it in one corner of your being. When you have done this you will understand the insignificance of the sensible in comparison with the greatness of the intelligible. Then the spiritual substance will be before your eyes, comprehending you and superior to you, and you will see your own being as though you were that substance.[7]

Plotinus suggests shaping your imaginings like the sculptor Pygmalion.

> Withdraw into yourself and look. And if you do not find yourself beautiful yet, act as does the creator of a statue that is to be made beautiful; he cuts away here, he smoothes there, he makes this line lighter, this other purer, until a lovely face has

---

6 *The Enneads of Plotinus,* trans. Grace H. Turnbull (Whitefish, MT: Kessinger Publishing, 2010), 5.5. 8.

7 Isaac Husik, *A History of Mediaeval Jewish Philosophy* (New York: The MacMillan Company, 1916), 69.

grown upon his work. So do you also; cut away
all that is excessive, straighten all that is crooked,
bring light to all that is in shadow; labor to make
all one glow of beauty and never cease chiseling
your statue until there shall shine out on you from
it the godlike splendor of virtue, until you shall
see the perfect goodness established in the stain-
less shrine.[8]

Ramana Maharshi, a Hindu mystic of the twentieth
century, gives a personal testimony of his search for
truth.

I am now seventy-four years old. And yet I
feel that I am an infant. I feel clearly that in spite
of all the changes I am a child. My Guru told me;
that child, which is you even now, is your real self.
Go back to that state of pure being, where the "I
am'" is still in its purity before it got contaminat-
ed with "this I am" or "that I am." Your burden
is of false self-identifications—abandon them all.
My Guru told me—"Trust me. I tell you; you are
divine. Take it as the absolute truth. Your joy is divine, your suffering is divine too. All comes from
God. Remember it always. You are God, your will
alone is done." I did believe him and soon realized how wonderfully true and accurate were his
words. I did not condition my mind by thinking:
"I am God, I am wonderful, I am beyond." I simply followed his instruction, which was to focus
the mind on pure being "I am," and stay in it. I
used to sit for hours together, with nothing but the
"I am" in my mind and soon peace and joy and a
deep all-embracing love became my normal state.
In it all disappeared—myself, my Guru, the life

8 Plotinus, *The Enneads*, translated by Stephen MacKenna (Bur-
dett, NY: Larson Publications, 1992), 64.

lived, the world around me. Only peace remained and unfathomable silence.[9]

The founder of Zen Buddhism, Bodhidharma, reminds us that the knowledge of truth is not far away. We are immersed in it. He also describes the effect of the experience of truth on a human being.

> Not knowing how near the Truth is,
> People seek It far away — what a pity!
> They are like one who, in the midst of water,
> Cries imploringly for a drink of water,
> Or like the son of a rich man
> Who wanders away among the poor...
> Those who testify to the truth of the nature of
>   the Self,
> Have found it by reflecting within themselves,
> And have gone beyond the realm of mere
>   ideas.
> For them opens the gate of the oneness of
>   cause and effect;
> And straight runs the path of non-duality...
> Abiding with the Undivided amidst the
>   divided,
> Whether going or returning, they remain
>   forever unmoved.
> Holding fast to, and remembering,
> That which is beyond thought,
> In their every act, they hear the voice of the
>   Truth.
> How limitless the sky of unbounded freedom!
> How pure the perfect moonlight of Wisdom!
> At that moment, what do they lack?
> As the eternally quiescent Truth reveals Itself
>   to them,

---

9 *I am That: Talks with Sri Nisargadatta Maharai*, trans. Maurice Frydman (Durham, NC: Acorn Press, 1982), 239.

This very earth is the lotus-land of Purity,
And this body is the body of the Buddha.[10]

---

10 D. T. Suzuki, *Essays in Zen Buddhism* (New York: Grove Press, 1961), 336.

WHAT IS ETERNAL LIFE? — DESIRE FOR LIFE

THE second basic desire is the desire for life. We do everything we can to hang on to life as we understand it. Death is a dark unknown. Does death mean a complete halt to consciousness, a vanishing of the sensations and impressions that constitute our experience of the world? Do we simply disappear, leaving behind only a decaying husk? Our substance does return to the earth from which it was composed. But what about our awareness, our sense of being, the *I am*? Is that snuffed out like a candle?

We have testimony from those who have experienced clinical death and revived. Even when the brain has shut down, near-death survivors report that they continue to observe what is happening. They are able to report details of medical procedures that happened while their bodies were comatose. Though scientists are skeptical, there seems to be evidence that when the body dies, the mind continues to function.

Our desire for life makes us hope that death of the body is not the end, that we can continue to live. We might imagine an afterlife, a heaven or hell, or some sort of continuation of consciousness. The Sufis say that after death there is a continuity with the life we have experienced in the body. They warn that it is easier to make changes in this life, to resolve old issues, to strive toward our ideal, and to find more happiness. They advise taking advantage of the short time we have in this world to prepare for the world to come. There you will live in the psychic world you have created for yourself, either accidentally or deliberately.

However, life beyond this life does not fully satisfy our deep desire for life. Even that disembodied life continues to change and evolve. What is it evolving toward? The ultimate goal of the desire for life is eternal life.

Just as the true unitary Reality is incomprehensible to the mind, so eternal life cannot fully be grasped. We understand duration only through our notion of time. That notion depends on change. We observe time passing by tracking changes around us: the rhythm of night and day resulting from the earth's rotation, the period of a pendulum, and the radiation frequency for a specific atomic transition in the cesium atom, used as the U.S. national standard of time.

Consider the state of universal intelligence that underlies and animates all life. One of the implications of a unitary state of intelligence is that it is perfect. It cannot be improved. But if it is already perfect, then it is unchanging. And if it is unchanging, then it exists outside of time. One could say that eternal life, in spite of the name, is an unchanging life that is timeless. There is no distinction between past, present, and future for eternal life. There is no passing of time. It is life freed from the tyranny of time, freed from decay and loss. One could say that primal intelligence enters the flow of time, but also never leaves the timeless state.

Since the universal intelligence is what animates us, it is our true life. Though our minds function entirely within the frame of time, yet our deeper, more essential life is timeless. In other words, we exist both within the stream of time and also in the silent timeless state. Without seeking it, we are already in a state of eternal life. In fact, we have never left that state.

Though this thought may give a little comfort, the catch is that without experiencing eternal life directly, it means little to us, and the fear and threat of death remains.

What can you do to get beyond the fear of death? Taking a cue from a saying of Prophet Muhammad, "Die before you die," the Sufis pretend to die while still alive, to find out what it means.

Once, on a spiritual retreat, I lay down on the floor and imagined that I had died. I saw my lifeless body. I saw grieving family gathered around the body. I witnessed a funeral service. Memories of me were recalled, and goodbyes were said. I saw my body disposed of, and my belongings given away or discarded. Over time, I saw that memories of me faded and my family and friends went on with their lives. Gradually, my influence and presence faded from the world. I felt relieved and freed from responsibilities.

The Buddhists practice more vivid confrontations with death. Whether meditating in a cemetery, handling human bones, or imagining the details of a decaying body, they overcome feelings of repulsion toward death and decay.

When you can release attachments to possessions, to relationships, and to the demands of the ego, you begin to free yourself from the urgency of time. Discovering peace and ease is a way to stop time, to deeply relax. There is a feeling of returning home after a long absence.

Once again we return to the same frontier. We are challenged to awaken from a bad dream. We cling to a fictional identity, knowing that one day it will be snatched from us. Like the man in the Buddhist parable, we hang on to the limb of a tree through the night, sure there is an abyss below us, only to find in the dawn that the ground is a foot beneath our feet. We suffer from a lack of faith in our true nature, which is immune to death. We can't *should* ourselves into having faith. What is gained in seeking your purpose in life is greater faith, discovery of a greater dimension of self, and willingness to loosen the grip of fear and embrace what life and death bring.

TRUE EMPOWERMENT — DESIRE FOR POWER

WHEN we speak about power, we usually mean will power. There are two steps involved in acting with power; first, making a decision and then exerting your will to carry it out. Making a decision may be rational or intuitive. Where does the initiative to exert your will originate?

We know how the brain sends a signal through the nervous system to move a muscle. But between making a decision about how to act and sending the signals that will initiate the action, there is a mysterious *go forward* step that is not simply mechanical. Will power seems like a gift of empowerment whose origin is a mystery. The effectiveness of our power in the world depends on our openness to this gift. If our receiver is open to a narrow band, our power is small.

There is another factor at play. Our power to accomplish may be thwarted by a larger power; for example, the power of a community or organization, the power of nature, or the power of unforeseen circumstances. There is a power at work that is larger than any individual. The scientist might call it *the power of circumstance*, which arises without any particular intent. The religious person might call it *God's Will*, directing the course of events according to a divine plan beyond our understanding. How can we understand this according to the ideas developed in this book? Imagine that the universal intelligence is seeking to unfold its hidden treasures in every individual. To manage this unimaginably complex puzzle, it brings its will to bear not only through individuals and communities, but also through all aspects of nature, the living creatures, and even the primal elements. All the circumstances that overwhelm individual wills then represent the universal will achieving its ends.

There is an art to discerning the universal will in action and finding a way to harmonize the personal will with it. Learning to open our receiver to let in the gift of will power involves coming to believe in oneself. A strong will usually goes hand in hand with a certain kind of personal confidence. As long as will power is motivated by personal needs and goals, it is likely sooner or later to be defeated by the personal will power of another or the universal will power.

There is a way to harmonize with the larger will by relaxing your grip on having things go your way. If you are driven, you might find yourself trying to force your way toward your goal. By exercising patience, relaxing, and consulting intuition about the direction to take, you can begin to sense the way things around you are flowing. Earlier in this book, I have referred to a sense of flow. There is an expression, *to be in the flow,* which conveys the idea of harmonizing with a larger perspective. When you trust the will of the guiding intelligence even more than you trust your personal will, then your power greatly expands. It is a power that may involve putting others before yourself. Nevertheless, it is a greater and more effective power than you can wield in your personal interest.

The impersonal will that comes through, is it an overwhelming power that destroys whatever stands in its way? We can get an idea of how this power works by looking at a few well known exemplars.

Consider the power and influence of modern figures such as Mahatma Gandhi and Martin Luther King, Jr. They renounced force yet went up against opponents of great power. By the measure of worldly force, their causes seemed hopeless. Yet they prevailed because the power they brought to bear was the power of love and truth. The power of their inspiration drew wide support, and the arraying of physical force against them only hastened the defeat of their opponents.

Consider how the power of an obscure itinerant preacher two thousand years ago, who taught only briefly and was ridiculed and publicly executed, has influenced half the world's population toward greater love and forgiveness.

The desire for power can be satisfied when you open wide the channel of your will, and discover there the love that embraces all souls and all creatures. This impersonal love is irresistible. In this love is the fulfillment of the desire for power.

Elusive Happiness — Desire for Joy

We humans play the game of "if only I had so and so, then I could be happy." When we acquire what we thought we must have, the thought of that object gets lost in the longing for the next object that promises happiness. We might as well admit it: we are never satisfied. Nothing, it seems, can give lasting happiness. Our sensitivity to the magic of what has beguiled us inevitably dulls, and the curse of accommodation transforms the desired object from gold to a copper penny. If it is pleasure we seek, afterwards we come to know the price we paid for it.

Yet the desire for happiness, despite repeated disappointments, never leaves us. Where can lasting happiness be found?

Are we taking life too seriously? There is a delight in humor that can take the edge off the frustration of elusive happiness.

Woody Allen has a knack for making fun of life's miseries.

> To love is to suffer. To avoid suffering one must not love. But then one suffers from not loving. Therefore, to love is to suffer; not to love is to suffer; to suffer is to suffer. To be happy is to love. To be happy, then, is to suffer, but suffering makes one

> unhappy. Therefore, to be happy one must love or love to suffer or suffer from too much happiness.[1]

And this contribution is from the poet W. H. Auden,

> We are all here on earth to help others; what on earth the others are here for I don't know.[2]

Auden's funny juxtaposition reminds us that happiness is elusive when we seek it for ourselves. When we help others, even without any external reward, we feel a satisfaction. This satisfaction is one feeling that we don't come to take for granted. It continues to bring us moments of happiness.

However, when we start to think about the needs of others and open our hearts to the scope of that need, we become aware of the unbearable load of suffering and injustice in the world. How can we ever be happy when so many live constantly in deprivation or suffer abuse? Those precious moments in life when happiness is showered on us—for example, falling in love, the birth of a baby, celebrating a victory over great odds—can we fully savor those experiences when our hearts are open to the desperate needs of others?

Woody Allen pinpointed the dilemma in an earlier quote. Happiness depends on opening the heart, but having a loving heart exposes one to suffering. How can happiness and suffering be reconciled?

The Sufis recognize a profound archetype: the broken heart. They understand it not only as a condition of individuals, but as a state of the universal intelligence. Departing from a state of perfection, entering duality, and animating the multitude of living creatures, intelligence opens itself to experience loss, guilt, remorse,

---

1 Woody Allen, *Love and Death* (MGM Studio Film, 1975).
2 Cited by W. H. Auden and attributed to John Foster Hall, English comedian.

and despair. It opens itself to every form of suffering. Thus it enters the state of the broken heart.

Does that mean that the desire for happiness can never be fulfilled? The nature of duality is that it is constantly in flux. Everything has its birth, its fullness, and its decline. When it fades away, where does it go? It dissolves back into the state of unity, the ocean of purity and perfection. The suffering the broken heart feels will not last. This too shall pass and return to perfection. All wounds will heal. All injustices will be resolved. All wrongs will be righted.

You can grow into lasting happiness through stages. In the first stage, you realize that you have prejudiced most choices and decisions in your own favor. Seeing the unfairness of your bias, you try to balance your actions more in favor of others. The greater balance helps you to feel more just.

In the next stage, you begin to see that your selfishness has been blind. There is a better selfishness, one that is more beneficial to yourself and others. You notice that actions have a reciprocal response. In common parlance, what goes out comes back. A generous act begets generosity back; a mean action boomerangs back upon the actor. As you give more generously of yourself, you begin to feel that life is more benevolent.

In the third stage, there comes a time when you discover that the greatest pleasure you can have is pleasure in the pleasure of another. A Sufi saint enjoyed his favorite dishes much more when others were pleased with them than when he ate them himself. At this stage you realize that the joys you seek for yourself pale beside the happiness you feel by pleasing another. You wish for very little for yourself but look for the opportunity to be of service.

This progression of insight and experience goes hand in hand with the opening and softening of the heart. When you experience more and more the pain of the broken heart, you can remain happy even through tears, knowing that every soul is destined for comfort and relief as it returns home and discards the burdens it has carried. As the shadow of your own burdens lifts, as the solidity of the presumed self thins, and the true self sends forth its rays, you come to realize that lasting happiness is not only possible, it is your birthright.

THE PEACE THAT SURPASSES UNDERSTANDING — DESIRE FOR PEACE

WHEN stress builds up from pressure, worry, too much activity, or too much emotion, we seek relief in something that distracts us. The possibilities for distraction have greatly expanded in recent times. We have been raised on a rich diet of sensation and stimulation. The nervous system accommodates as the level of stimulation increases, and, over time, we need more extreme stimulation for the same degree of gratification. We especially feed the mind, which is so overstimulated that it rarely gets a chance to rest. We don't know how to give the mind a rest. When we want to have peace and quiet, the mind chatters on, and we find it difficult to calm it down.

We have a deep-felt need for peace. The Sufis say that peace begins with better breathing. We generally regard breathing as automatic and don't pay much attention to it. The manner of our breathing reflects the state of agitation or relaxation we happen to be in. Trying to control breathing interferes with its natural rhythm. However, simple awareness of breathing brings about a change, which in turn contributes to a state of relaxation. If you notice how you are breathing, without judgment, very soon the breath by itself becomes deeper, slower, and more relaxed. You may find yourself sighing. When each breath becomes deeper, notice how it affects your body. You may find that your muscles are relaxing. What happens in the pit of the stomach where tension is often held? What about the neck and face? Breathing well and consciously is the first step to finding peace.

Next, close your eyes while still being aware of relaxed breathing. Pay attention to your body, and consciously release muscles that feel tight or held. Let the abdomen expand. Sit up straight and let the shoulders down. Imagine the blood circulating through the limbs and the torso, spreading a feeling of warmth.

Chances are that you will enjoy a peaceful feeling for a few minutes before you notice the mind trying to get your attention. When thoughts begin to distract you, imagine a bright light inside your head. Make it an intense and attractive light. Let yourself be absorbed in it. Imagine it is the light of your consciousness. Relax your body again and begin to draw the light down into the body until it is filled with light.

Now there is a further step in relaxation. There is a subtle tension that we hardly notice. In common speech, we call it *holding myself together*. Without realizing it, we are constantly orienting ourselves to our physical, mental, and emotional environment to see *who am I in this place*? Can you deliberately relax this subtle tension? It means letting go of holding yourself together, letting go of your identity. It can be a great relief to be nobody. It feels like floating in space. You are free of every pressure to be something. Enjoy being empty.

We feel we have to be somebody to impress others so they will like us or notice us. Otherwise, we might be rejected or ignored. However, it is our true nature to be filled by spirit when we make room for it. Our trying to be somebody fills up a capacity we have that would otherwise be receiving a fresh influx of life. If we could only trust in the perpetual infusion of new life, we could more and more relax the tension that keeps us bound to our habits and cramped self-image.

We have become accustomed to stress as a way of life. We take it as the way life is. We are also used to seeking stimulation. We've forgotten our natural state in the blur of artificially induced excitation. What is our natural state? It is a feeling of peace and relaxation. When we withdraw from stimulation and relax deeply, our initial reaction may be boredom or impatience. We may hope for relief from stress only to find a vague feeling of drifting in space. The mind tries to be helpful by proposing entertainments or by reminding us of pressing projects that need our attention. The heart cautions us that we are not through with unresolved feelings and pulls us back into a world of emotion. Your reaction to silence and emptiness may be resistance. But what if you turned that attitude around and welcomed the unknown? What if you entered the silence with a feeling of expectant joy? What if you imagined that this is the path taking you to your long lost home? Instantly you would feel the promise of peace.

The desire for peace is a deep need, and nothing in this world can satisfy it. When we try to relax and open up to our natural condition, we become aware of how tightly caught we are in habits of escaping. We see how addicted we are to stimulation of all kinds.

Let that agitation settle. Sink down into stillness, at the same time rising to meet its promise. The peace that surpasses understanding wishes to reveal itself to you.

Serving One, Serving All

WHEN the attractions and pursuits of life lose their appeal, when you become weary of life's rewards, the deeper desire for knowledge, life, power, happiness, and peace remain. By turning inward, a new path of accomplishment opens up. But does this turning inward make you more self-absorbed? Does it make you more isolated and build higher the walls of separation from our fellow creatures?

On the contrary, as we have seen, the path to satisfying the deeper needs of the soul leads to what Pir Vilayat Inayat Khan has called *a breakdown which avers itself to be a breakthrough.* As you come to know yourself more deeply, you discover that the secrets that satisfy your deepest needs are hidden behind the stubborn persistence of your meager self-concept. The greater knowledge of who you are is waiting to reveal itself to you. To make room for it means releasing the grip of separation and isolation. Turning inward can lead you to feel closer to your fellow humans by discovering in yourself and others what is universal.

The false self, which I have contended is no more than a concept, yet has a life of its own. It clings desperately to that life. If you battle with the ego, you may find yourself ever more drawn into self-absorption. The Sufis picture the ego as a wild horse, stubborn, self-assertive, and resistant to training. Who can train such a wild animal? You can't train yourself by trying to lift yourself by your own bootstraps. First, you need to stop identifying with the ego. The wayward small self is meant to be your servant, not your equal or, worse, your master. When you are lifted up by remembering your ideals, you are ennobled. It is your noble self that can witness the bucking and kicking of the ego and strongly rein it in.

Taking the path of liberation, by diving deep into the mystery at the core of your existence, starts by unlearning who you thought you were. Then you float in a kind of nether realm until your heart opens, and your longing carries you into knowing, into eternal life, into the irresistible power of love, into innate happiness, and into enduring peace.

As the false self loosens its grip on you, you find that the *I* that remains is the same universal intelligence that inhabits every living thing. You begin to see that same familiar intelligence and loving nature peeking through the personalities of those you encounter in life. The idiosyncrasies, the behaviors you react to and judge, seem less important than the bond of universal life that is always present. Isolation and separation are dissolving. Whatever you gain for yourself seems evanescent and not of much value. What you can do for others is more rewarding.

The gift of life itself seems so overwhelming that you look for ways to give something back to the source of life. However small it may be, yet it gives you happiness when there is some way you can give back. In serving others, you are serving the intelligence that is animating the other; and yet, in essence, is the same as you.

Seeking the purpose of life begins by trusting the desires that motivate you, and learning that there is a universal spirit behind your desire, helping you to accomplish it. The path of sadhana or achievement, culminates by tracing the path of desire to its conclusion, and learning that ultimate satisfaction in life comes from serving the living spirit in all.

But there is no need to rush through the journey. Each step is of great value. The joy of this adventure is in the process. Do not judge where you are on this path. Take the step that is before you, trusting that the guidance and support will be there as you progress.

The intelligence that is behind this great enterprise has a sense of humor. At the same time it is a most playful spirit, a most serious spirit, and a wise and loving spirit.

Afterword

WHILE on a tour of the United States in 1926, Hazrat Inayat Khan visited industrialist Henry Ford. A reporter who hoped to have a few minutes with the Sufi mystic waited outside Henry Ford's office and approached Inayat Khan as he left the office. The reporter knew he had only a short time to ask a question so he chose it carefully.

He asked, "Mr. Khan, what is the purpose of life?"

Inayat Khan answered, "Ultimately there is no purpose."

The reporter countered, "Then why do you travel so far to give your teachings?"

Inayat Khan's answer was, "When you have great joy, then you would like to share it with others."

About the Author

William Hassan Suhrawardi Gebel spent his under-graduate years at Johns Hopkins University, graduating with a BA in physics. He received a PhD in astrophysics from the University of Wisconsin and did postdoctoral work at the University of Chicago's Yerkes Observatory. He was an assistant professor of astrophysics at SUNY Stony Brook. Leaving academia in 1971, he joined the Theater Workshop school in Boston and then Omega Theater acting company. He performed in original shows created by the theater company and participated in several performances of the *Cosmic Celebration*, a pageant created by Pir Vilayat Inayat Khan and Saphira Linden. W. H. S. Gebel then worked as a technical writer until his children were grown and left the nest. Subsequently completing an MA in counseling psychology from Lesley University, he worked as a psychotherapist at Windhorse Associates in Northampton, Massachusetts. For eight years he served as Secretary General of the Sufi Order International, working closely with Pir Zia Inayat-Khan until retirement in 2012.